THE CHINESE IN SAN FRANCISCO

A Pictorial History

LAVERNE MAU DICKER

Curator of Photographs, California Historical Society,
San Francisco

With a Preface by
Thomas W. Chinn, Chinese Historical Society of America
San Francisco

Dover Publications, Inc.
New York

In memory of
TERRY WM. MANGAN

Published in Canada by General Publishing Company, Ltd., 30 Lesmill Road, Don Mills, Toronto, Ontario.
Published in the United Kingdom by Constable and Company, Ltd., 10 Orange Street, London WC2H 7EG.

The Chinese in San Francisco: A Pictorial History is a new work, first published by Dover Publications, Inc., in 1979.

Book Design by Carol Belanger Grafton

International Standard Book Number: 0-486-23868-7
Library of Congress Catalog Card Number: 79-50669

Manufactured in the United States of America
Dover Publications, Inc.
180 Varick Street
New York, N.Y. 10014

Preface

This book introduces a new dimension in presenting Chinese-American history. In the 125-plus years since the discovery of gold in California, the public has had to rely on the written word, or the pen and ink sketches of early-day illustrators, for information on the Chinese in America. Since the advent of photography, there seems to have been no publication of a serious chronological series of photographs such as this.

This initial effort, as the author herself acknowledges, is but a first small step forward in presenting Chinese-American history through photographs. It is, however, an important step, and therefore a few explanatory remarks are in order as to what the reader should try to find and interpret here.

If you are coming to the subject for the first time, you may want to read the entire text carefully, to familiarize yourself with the background of the Chinese. Then, as you go through the pictures, you will more readily understand the segments of their history.

From the very beginning you will see their travails—from leaving a homeland that was devastated with flood, famine and strife, and offered little more than mere existence, to their travels and sojourn in a new and foreign land where language, dress and custom set them worlds apart.

In their struggles to eke out a livelihood, and to send a little money back to their families, they endured a life of untold sacrifice—a story yet to be written in depth.

Throughout these years of hardship, the Chinese have tried to live up to the teachings of those sages who set down the rules for exemplary conduct. These teachings guided their every action for more than a century, and even today play a considerable part in their lives and behavior.

History records only inadequately some of the privations of these sojourners in the gold mines and in the many variegated types of labor they performed. Only in a few instances, such as the building of the first transcontinental railroad, was their work acknowledged in a small measure.

Later, as California grew, as jobs and opportunities declined and anti-Chinese activities increased, these people gradually retreated into those enclaves known as Chinatowns.

San Francisco's Chinatown became the acknowledged "headquarters" for these industrious but little understood people. Following America's first exclusion act in 1882—directed against the Chinese—their fate seemed to be sealed and they seemed destined to disappear.

By 1921 their numbers had dwindled to 61,000, a great part of these confined to a few square blocks in San Francisco. It is on this area that the author chose to focus her book. It was in San Francisco's Chinatown that the major transformations affecting their future took place. In this book you will find the untold story of a magnificent struggle by a small minority, living through its fears and hopes, to become a most valuable part of the population of a world-renowned city. Refusing to be daunted, they brought into being a true city within a city. You will see in the pictures how totally involved they became in the struggle for existence. Accepted only with severe limitations outside of their Chinatown, they created their own world and their own activities which sustained them. It is literally true that a man could be born in Chinatown, live there all his life and die without ever having set foot outside of this community, so diversified were the capabilities of the "inner city."

With the turn of the century, and especially after

the 1906 earthquake and fire had "purged" China-town of its lawless elements, a new generation with a new spirit came into being: the American-born (only a tiny handful of families had begotten children earlier). No longer were all eyes constantly turned to the homeland in faraway China. Now the freedom that they found, the opportunity to seek goals here that they would never know in China, permeated their very being. They wanted to become a part of America. It became fashionable to be patriotic. A few Chinese-Americans served in World War I, and some made the supreme sacrifice.

The past half-century has brought about a justification for all the sacrifices that had been undergone. Pride in accomplishment became a growing symbol.

As we peruse these pages and study the photos, a growing sense of empathy comes into being. Each one of these pictures does actually speak ten thousand words. And the text provides the setting for each series of photographs—enhancing the whole.

In the view of this writer, who has been active in the San Francisco Chinese community for more than a half-century, Mrs. Laverne Mau Dicker has performed a valuable service in presenting this volume. It should do much to solve some of the vexing problems of interpreting parts of our history which cannot be readily put down in words.

THOMAS W. CHINN

Introduction

The Chinese, from the beginning, were different from other immigrant groups because they never intended to settle permanently in America. Their story, therefore, is not a typical immigrant history. Since the Gold Rush days, the Chinese in California have faced unbelievable hardships: set apart from the mainstream of society by their customs and appearance, they were abused, vilified and hunted down like animals. They are the only ethnic group in the history of the United States to have been specifically denied entrance into the country.

Yet in the past hundred years the public's attitude toward the Chinese in America has undergone a significant change. In 1878 the Chinese were regarded as ignorant, untrustworthy heathens; today, both the Postmaster of San Francisco and the California Secretary of State are Chinese-Americans. This change is also reflected in *Reader's Guide to Periodic Literature* titles through the years: "Why the Chinese Should Be Excluded" (1902), "Born American, But—" (1926), "Municipal Positions Wanted for Capable Educated Chinese" (1943), "Our Amazing Chinese Kids" (1955) and "Success Story of One Minority Group in the U.S." (1966).

Why the 180-degree turn? What factors contributed to this, and how gradual was the change? What was life in Chinatown like in the past, as compared to now? These are questions I sought to answer in this book.

San Francisco was the most logical city on which to focus. During the Gold Rush, San Francisco was California's major port and played host to all new arrivals, and in later years, the Pacific Mail Steamship Lines established regular routes between China and San Francisco. Today, the city possesses the largest Chinatown in the United States.

In no way is the present volume intended as an in-depth history of the Chinese in San Francisco. Those readers interested in such a work should refer to *A History of the Chinese in California* (Chinese Historical Society of America, 1969), which I found to be the most complete source of its kind, or to the selected bibliography at the end of this volume. The text of this book is, rather, a framework for the photographs, which tell their own story. There are consequently no footnotes; however, all sources used may be found in the bibliography.

It is indeed fortunate that the major wave of Chinese immigration began as late as it did—1848—because by then photography was practiced widely. Amateur photographers as well as such "name" photographers as Taber and Genthe were drawn to the Chinese quarter of the city by the colorful sights—the outdoor markets and bazaars—and by the curious customs and dress of the people. Thus, even though the original quarter was demolished by the fire and earthquake of 1906, an excellent visual record of the Chinese in San Francisco still exists.

The subject matter of this book is not strictly limited to San Francisco, for any history of the Chinese in San Francisco must necessarily include discussions of Chinese activities in other geographical areas. Mining and railroad construction, for example, both had a direct effect on the history of the Chinese in San Francisco. The photographs are arranged roughly in chronological order, though there will inevitably be some time overlaps.

Special thanks are in order to a number of people who went out of their way to assist with the preparation of this book: to Thomas W. Chinn of the Chinese Historical Society of America for the use of his personal collection, for his expert advice and guidance, and for his insightful preface; to Bill Robertson of the Southern Pacific Transportation Company, Brian Suen of the Oakland Museum and Deborah Ginberg of the Society of California Pioneers for their patient assistance; to Bertha Hing, Allen Y. Lew and Ruth Haw for kindly supplying me with information about the Genthe photo "Children of High Class"; to Gloria Silberstein Brown for making her collection of photographs available to me; to my father, William H. Mau, for helping me to unravel linguistic puzzles and historical problems; to Gary Kurutz and the rest of my colleagues at the California Historical Society for their staunch support; to my editor, Stanley Appelbaum; and most of all to my husband Kelly for his never-ending help and encouragement.

Contents

Early Immigration and Mining

[PICTURE PAGES 29–32]

It has been suggested that the Chinese visited the California coast centuries before the arrival of the Europeans. As early as the fifth century A.D., Chinese texts described a land called Fusang which lay some seven thousand miles east of Japan and which some researchers interpret to be Baja California or Mexico. There are stories of Chinese junks landing at Monterey and Mendocino, and in 1774 Juan Bautista de Anza, a pioneer Mexican explorer of Alta California, reported seeing there a shipwreck of unfamiliar construction.

A frustrating lack of documentary evidence, however, makes it impossible to pinpoint the arrival of the first Chinese in California. The San Francisco *Chronicle* of July 21, 1878, stated that a Cantonese merchant named Chum Ming arrived in San Francisco in 1847 and was instrumental in spreading news of the discovery of gold among his countrymen. Other sources claim that the first Chinese—two men and a woman—arrived with the Charles V. Gillespie family on the American brig *Eagle* on February 2, 1848, although the ship's passenger list does not corroborate this claim.

Suffice it to say that in all probability there were already Chinese in and around San Francisco when gold was discovered at Sutter's Mill in January of 1848. Certainly they were there several months later, for the San Francisco *Star* of April 1, 1848, mentioned the presence of "two or three 'Celestials' ... who found ready employment."

China at this time was undergoing a period of tremendous upheaval. Following her defeat by Britain in the Opium War of 1840, a reluctant China was forced into trade with the West, and native handicraft industries—notably textiles—suffered from the increased importation of Western goods. The Manchu dynasty, which had ruled over China since the mid-seventeenth century, was fraught with corruption. From 1846 to 1850 floods and droughts throughout China resulted in widespread famine in the already overpopulated country. Banditry and local warfare were common, and there were many peasant rebellions. In 1851 the T'ai-p'ing Rebellion, the greatest uprising against the Manchus, broke out. This war was to last thirteen years, claim millions of lives and lay waste large areas of southeastern China before being crushed by the Manchus and their Western allies.

Understandably, during the late 1840's and early 1850's, many Chinese eagerly seized the opportunity to seek their fortunes in California, which was referred to colloquially as *Gum San*, or (Land of the) Golden Mountain. By the end of 1851 there were an estimated 4,000 Chinese in California; by the next year their numbers had increased to 25,000.

Chinese immigration to the United States took three major forms. The credit-ticket system advanced passage to the emigrant on the condition that he repay the debt out of his earnings after reaching his destination. Under the contract-labor system, an American company paid for transportation, in return for which the emigrant agreed to work for the company for a specified number of years; the price of passage was then deducted from his wages. The coolie trade* was essentially a system of slave labor, in which potential workers were kidnapped or tricked into signing false contracts. (Illegal in most parts of the United States, this trade was prevalent in Peru and Cuba.) The majority of Chinese migrated to California on the credit-ticket system.

* The word "coolie" is of Indian–East Pakistani origin. It was adapted by the Chinese into the appropriate *k'u-li*, which means "bitter strength."

The average trans-Pacific crossing took 62 days, and conditions aboard ship frequently resembled those on an African slave vessel: immigrants were crowded into the holds like cattle, ill-fed and harshly treated. There were often riots and murders. On the *Robert Browne*, which left Amoy for San Francisco in 1852, members of the crew and some officers amused themselves by cutting off the queues of the Chinese passengers. The passengers rebelled, killed the captain and officers, and ran the ship aground east of Formosa. The *Libertad*, after an ill-fated 50-day voyage from Hong Kong in 1854, arrived in San Francisco with 100 of its 500 Chinese passengers dead.

Prior to 1860, only 8% of the Chinese population in California resided in San Francisco; most departed immediately for the mines. The San Francisco daily *Alta California* of May 3, 1852, observed:

> For the last few days our streets have swarmed with Chinese, on their way to the southern mines. ... The southern country will soon be alive with them whether their advent prove beneficial or not.

The early Chinese miners were a picturesque sight in their customary attire of blue cotton knee-length tunics, baggy blue trousers, broad-brimmed hats and wooden shoes. They learned quickly that it was wiser not to compete with white miners for the richest claims, and instead operated in worked-over areas or unpromising sites, using the most primitive of mining methods. Two men would shovel, while another rocked the box so that the heavier gold particles settled to the bottom. The pan and rocker were simple pieces of equipment, easily carried. Because the Chinese worked in groups—usually a dozen or more, for protection—they were able to bare large sections of stream bed by constructing wing dams. A visitor described one such dam as being "two or three hundred yards in length ... built of large pine trees" and noted that "in handling such immense logs they [the Chinese] are exceedingly ingenious in applying mechanical power, particularly ... the force of a large number of men upon one point."

Initially, when there were few Chinese in the mines, they were regarded with amused tolerance. As their numbers increased, however, so did the hostility against them. There already existed a great deal of anti-foreign feeling and color prejudice in the mining country, intensified by the presence of American Southerners, who made up one-third of California's population in those early years. South Americans, Polynesians, Frenchmen and Spaniards alike were considered "colored," and in 1850 a Foreign Miner's License tax law was enacted. Principally aimed at Spanish and South American miners—the law was printed in both English and Spanish and circulated throughout the mining districts—this ordinance required that all persons not native-born citizens of the United States buy a license to mine at the rate of $20 per month. The result of the law was the immediate depopulation of the mining camps. San Francisco was crowded with bankrupt foreigners, and the Chilean consul provided homeward passage for 800 miners. Obviously a failure as a moneymaker, the Foreign Miners License tax law was repealed in 1851.

Mary Roberts Coolidge, an early sociologist at Stanford University, emphasized in her book *Chinese Immigration* that even though there was a "violent, pro-American" movement in the early mining years, there was an "absence of specific anti-Chinese feeling before 1852." It was in 1852 that California Governor John Bigler delivered a speech terming the Chinese a danger to the welfare of the state. The same year, the insidious miner's tax was renewed at the rate of $3 per month, with the collector receiving 10%. Any person hiring foreigners to work in the mines was also liable. Although there was no direct mention of the Chinese in the law, it was clear who the targets were. In 1853 the tax was raised to $4 a month, the collector's commission was raised to 15%, and tax collectors were given the authority to seize and sell the property of debtors at one hour's notice. In 1855 the law was printed in Spanish, French and Chinese, and provisions were made for the tax to be increased by $2 per month in each succeeding year. At a time when most Chinese miners were earning, on the average, less than $6 per month, this was a most stringent tax.

There were even more serious threats than these financial harassments; a Chinese entering the mining districts literally took his life into his hands. The Shasta *Republican* of December 18, 1856, reported:

> Hundreds of Chinamen have been slaughtered in cold blood in the last five years by the desperadoes that infest our state. The murder of Chinamen was almost of daily occurrence; yet in all this time we have heard of but two or three cases where guilty parties were brought to justice. ... Many persons have avowed themselves opposed to the execution of white men for the murder of Chinamen.

An 1862 committee to the state legislature echoed:

> Eighty-eight Chinamen ... are known to have been murdered by white people, eleven of which number are known to have been murdered by Col-

lectors of Foreign-Miner's License Tax—sworn officers of the law. But two of the murderers have been convicted and hanged. Generally they have been allowed to escape without the slightest punishment.

Chinese miners were also preyed upon by bandits. Hubert Howe Bancroft, in his late nineteenth-century *History of California*, related that

> Chinamen ... usually walked to the mines, or travelled on Indian ponies; but returning, if they had treasure, they took the coach, and by this means frequently lost a whole season's profits.

Joaquín Murieta's band of outlaws was said to have killed Chinese "as hunters kill a covey of quail." The favorite pastime of Murieta's henchman Manuel García, better known as "Three-Finger Jack," was to tie a group of Chinese miners together by their queues and cut their throats. These atrocities gave rise to the expression "a Chinaman's chance," meaning no chance at all.

In some parts of California, the anti-Chinese factions resorted to threats of violence. Mariposa and other towns in the Agua Fria Creek district posted the following bill in 1856:

> Notice is hereby given to all Chinese in the Agua Fria and its tributaries, to leave within 10 days, from this date, and any failing to comply shall be subjected to 39 lashes and moved by the force of arms.

Nor could the harassed Chinese fight back in the courts. An 1850 law prevented Indians, Negroes or mulattos from giving evidence in any case involving a white person, and in 1854 Hugh C. Murray, Chief Justice of the California State Supreme Court, widened the definition of "Indian" to include the entire Mongolian race. As Mark Twain later wrote in *Roughing It*, "Any white man can swear a Chinaman's life away in the courts, but no Chinaman can testify against a white man."

As a result, the population in the mines declined as Chinese miners drifted toward the cities in search of less expensive, less dangerous occupations. By 1880, 30% of the Chinese in California were located in San Francisco, and the 1890 directory of Humboldt County (site of the northernmost gold fields in Gold Rush days) boasted that it was the "only county in California with no Chinamen."

Early Days in San Francisco

[PICTURE PAGES 33–44]

Like the Chinese in the mining country, the Chinese in San Francisco encountered little prejudice in the early days. It was not until years later, when immigration from China reached its peak, that hostility from the white community began to increase.

Possibly the first newspaper reference to the Chinese as a community appeared in the *Alta California* on August 26, 1850. There was a meeting in Portsmouth Square (then known as the Plaza) to which the "China Boys" were invited to receive Christian literature printed in Chinese.

> The Chinese are very anxious to turn out, and will muster very strong—probably 200 or 300—and the occasion cannot be otherwise than interesting. The dissemination of Scriptural truths among the members of a nation otherwise highly civilized is a great and good object; and when we consider the remarkable intelligence of the Chinese, their aptitude and capacity for acquiring knowledge, we cannot do less than believe that the happiest results will follow.

At the meeting, Justice Nathaniel Bennett delivered a speech noteworthy for its egalitarian theme:

> Born and raised under different Governments and speaking different tongues, we nevertheless meet here to-day as brothers. ... You stand among us in all respects as equals. ... Henceforth we have one country, one hope, one destiny.

Mayor John W. Geary, Rev. Albert Williams of the First Presbyterian Church and Rev. T. D. Hunt also spoke at the meeting. A-Hee, the self-appointed interpreter for the Chinese delegation, translated the proceedings for his countrymen, who were dressed in their finest holiday attire. Norman As-Sing, a colorful character who at the time was the undisputed leader of the Chinese in San Francisco, was also in attendance.

At the end of the ceremonies, the Mayor invited the Chinese to participate in memorial services to be held the following day for President Zachary Taylor. His invitation was accepted, and hundreds of Chinese in embroidered silk robes joined their fellow San Franciscans in the procession.

Several days later a letter, written by A-Hee and Norman As-Sing on behalf of the Chinese community, was printed in the *Alta California*. The letter, dated August 30 and addressed to the Mayor, read in part:

> The China-boys wish to thank you for the kind mark of attention you bestowed upon them in extending to them an invitation to join the citizens of San Francisco in doing honor to the memory of the late President of the United States, Gen. Zachary Taylor. ... The China-boys are fully sensible to the great loss this country has sustained in the death of its chieftain and ruler, and mourn with you. ... Strangers as they are among you, they kindly appreciate the many kindnesses received at your hands. ...

This was one of the few times that the California press showed the Chinese to be capable of putting together an intelligent sentence.

The Chinese in San Francisco also took part in California Admission Day ceremonies (October 1850, celebrating California's entrance into the Union), and the *Alta California* predicted buoyantly that "The China Boys will yet vote at the same polls, study at the same schools, and bow at the same altar as our countrymen." In 1852 Governor John McDougal recommended that land grants be given to the Chinese, whom he described as "one of the most worthy of our newly adopted citizens," to encourage immigration. When the San Francisco Committee of Vigilance was formed in 1856 to suppress the criminal elements in the town, Chinese merchants contributed generously to the cause and received an official vote of thanks.

San Francisco in the early days was a tented community of young men; the census of 1850 shows a female population of less than 8% of the total. Without women, even the simplest household tasks, such as cleaning and laundering, became monumental. San Francisco's lack of large amounts of fresh water only added to the problem.

Washerwoman's Lagoon, a body of fresh water located at the foot of Russian Hill two miles west of the then city limits, served as the largest "laundry" in the city, with the work being done mainly by Spanish and Indian women. However, the lagoon was not large enough to accommodate laundry for the entire populace. It was not uncommon for laundry to be sent by ship to Canton or Honolulu to be washed; it would be delivered to the owners by return steamer several months later. Because the going rate for washing, ironing and starching shirts was $8 per dozen, it was frequently a cheaper proposition to throw away soiled garments and buy new ones.

The Chinese, many of whom had been driven from the mines and were now badly in need of employment, saw the need and filled it. Opening a laundry took little capital: one needed only soap, a scrub board, an iron and an ironing board. Because laundrymen picked up and delivered, the business location was unimportant, and rent could be kept at a minimum. Two laundries sometimes shared the same premises, with one operating during the day and the other at night. Self-employment was an ideal solution for the Chinese, for it placed them in a position where they neither had to work for whites nor compete with them for jobs.

The price for laundering shirts dropped to $2 per dozen when the Chinese entered the business. So industrious were these early laundrymen that a traveler in San Francisco who wondered at the strange slapping noise was told, "You are in close proximity to Washerwoman's Bay, and I warn you to go no farther if you value your life, for the shirt buttons are flying thick."

The Chinese in California were prevented by circumstance from carrying on their traditional means of earning a living: farming or trading. The Workingmen's Party and anti-Chinese bias kept them out of the labor market, the unions kept them out of organized labor, the Alien Land Acts kept them from owning farms, the Foreign Miner's License tax kept them out of the mines. Laundries thus became a line of work peculiar to the Chinese in this country; it was their predominant occupation for well over half a century. By 1880, 7,500 Chinese in San Francisco were engaged in the laundry business; in 1920 an estimated 30% of all Chinese in the United States were employed in laundries.

Restaurants became another prevalent form of business among the Chinese in California, a "natural" business for a people who are traditionally brought up to appreciate fine cuisine and its preparation* and among whom "Have you eaten?" is an accepted form of greeting.

There were Chinese restaurants in San Francisco as early as 1849—a necessity at a time when few Chinese lodging houses included kitchen facilities, and emigrants longed for their native foods. These quickly became popular with white miners and provided a welcome change from their customary diet of bread and potatoes. Chinese food, although unfamiliar to the Western palate, was light, hot and tasty. It was thrifty for the restaurant owner (one pound of meat, cut up and cooked with bamboo shoots and mushrooms, fed several people), and nutritious for the patrons because it consisted mainly of lean meats and fresh vegetables.

There were fewer restaurants than laundries among the Chinese because they required a greater capital investment (location being important, rents were higher), a certain familiarity with the English language and better managerial skills. However, catering was a more stimulating form of work; restaurant workers were with people all day and generally found their lives less monotonous and lonely than did the solitary laundrymen.

Many Chinese turned to the fishing industry for sustenance after being driven from the mines. The January 21, 1854, issue of *Chamber's Journal* contained the following item:

> Many of our readers may not be aware that on the south side of Rincon Point [San Francisco] near the mouth of Mission Creek, there is a settlement of Chinese well worth a visit. It consists of about one hundred and fifty inhabitants, who are chiefly engaged in fishing. They have twenty-five boats. ... The fish which they catch consist of sturgeon ... and

* The philologist Lin Yutang wrote: "If there is anything the Chinese are serious about, it is neither religion nor learning, but food." Three great banquets mark milestones in the life of nearly every Chinese: at birth, marriage and death.

shark, and large quantities of herring. The latter are dried whole, while the larger are cut into thin pieces. When they are sufficiently dry, they are packed in barrels, boxes, or sacks, and sent into town to be disposed of to those of their countrymen who are going to the mines or are bound upon long voyages. ... The average yield ... a day was about three thousand pounds, and they find ready sale for them at five dollars the hundred pounds.

By 1870 Chinese fishing camps had been established down the coast from Oregon to Baja California. San Francisco was a major center.

Shrimp fishing was a related industry which provided hundreds of Chinese with employment; shrimp camps were clustered at Point Avisadera south of San Francisco, Point San Quentin, Point San Pedro and Tomales Bay in Marin County, and Point San Pablo in the East Bay. Using fine-mesh bag nets imported from China, Chinese fishermen brought in large quantities of shrimp, and by 1880 California ranked as one of the eight greatest shrimp-producing states in the country.

Abalone gathering, too, proved to be a profitable enterprise, though Americans at the time were unaware that abalone was edible. In 1880 alone, Chinese fishermen sold $38,800 worth of abalone meat and $88,800 worth of shells, which were shipped to China to be used in inlay work.

Even in fishing activities, however, the Chinese could not escape harassing regulations. In 1860 a tax of $4 per month was placed upon all Chinese fishermen. Refusal to pay resulted in seizure of boats and other equipment. This tax, unlike the Foreign Miner's Tax, was unsuccessful, and was repealed in 1864. In the mid-1870's a law was passed regulating the size of the mesh used in shrimp and drag nets, and in the 1880's another fishing tax law was enacted, establishing a $2.50 per month license fee. By that time, however, most Chinese had moved on to other occupations.

Very few of the Chinese who made their living in agriculture were independent farmers; the majority were sharecroppers (the landlord received one-half of the profits from vegetables and grain, and three-fifths of the fruit) who hired Chinese laborers. Chinese truck gardeners cultivated gardens outside the San Francisco city limits and sold their wares to local markets, also peddling vegetables door to door—a boon to housewives in the outlying districts.

During the same period of time when Chinese laundries were capitalizing on the need for domestic services and the scarcity of women in the West, many Chinese went into service in white households as cooks and servants. Their efficiency and loyalty soon became legendary; San Franciscans spoke fondly of "our faithful Sing" or "our cook Lum" and entrusted them with the running of their households and the raising of their children, sometimes for two or three generations. Good Chinese cooks and servants were much sought after and earned up to twice as much as their white or black counterparts. For the Chinese, in turn, working for a prosperous Caucasian family was a source of pride, a way of escaping the dreary atmosphere of Chinatown. They referred to their employers' households affectionately as *kwei lao*, or "devil's building" (Caucasians being designated as *fon kwei*, "foreign devil").

The Chinese in San Francisco were also involved in trade industries such as boots and shoes, cigars, brooms, candles and soap, clothing, cordage and whips. They gathered rags for the paper industry and worked as molders in iron factories. In the 1860's Agoston Haraszthy, the "father of California's wine industry," opened a new avenue of enterprise when he hired 100 Chinese to work in his vineyards and winery; many Chinese found employment in the wine country—Napa and Sonoma Counties—north of San Francisco, and became the preferred grapepickers in northern and central California vineyards.

There was hardly a field in which the Chinese were not employed. As George B. Morris stated in "The Chinaman as He is,"* "It would be eisier [sic] to enumerate the occupations in which the Chinese are not engaged than those in which they are."

* This illiterate handwritten manuscript at the Bancroft Library, Berkeley, undated but probably from the period around 1880, contains detailed, if biased, descriptions of the Chinese in California.

Chinese Women

[PICTURE PAGES 45–48]

Early Chinatown was notable for its lack of women. Between 1848 and 1854 only 16 out of 45,000 Chinese immigrants were women. The main reason for this was that the Chinese were not immigrants in the classic sense: they did not come to the United States with the intention of settling permanently. They were here strictly for economic betterment, to work and save enough money to return to China and buy land near their native village. Therefore, it was the breadwinners, the young husbands and fathers, who sailed to San Francisco; wives were expected to raise the children and keep the home, preparatory to the day the head of the household returned. Bachelor immigrants returned to China after a few years, married and stayed until an heir was born. They then went back to *Gum San*, leaving their new family behind.

The family was the basic unit of Chinese society. This was not the limited, or immediate, family group of today, but rather an extended family or clan. This concept served several purposes: in an agrarian society, as China was at the time, many hands were necessary to plant and harvest the crops. Also, such an extended kinship network offered protection to its members; there would always be a "cousin" to provide food or shelter in a crisis.

Thus, marriage was a family business, not an individual choice. The Reverend Otis Gibson, a Protestant minister who worked among the Chinese in San Francisco for many years, observed in his book *The Chinese in America* (1877):

> The betrothal, the arrangements for the marriage festivities and life settlement are all conducted for the children by the parents or guardians, with the help of a middle-man or go-between. ... Although our young people would rebel against the intro-duction of such a custom among us, yet it is doubtful whether the system ... in this country results in any better life settlements than those arranged for the inexperienced young people of China by their parents, who can use their judgment unmoved by fancy and romance.

Children—the continuation of the family—were the primary concern of a marriage. Sons were important because they would carry on the family name and tradition. Daughters were much less desirable because they were basically raised for the benefit of another family: once a woman married, she was considered a member of her husband's clan.

If any one word characterized the life of a Chinese woman, it was obedience. A woman traditionally spent her entire life subject to the wishes of some man, be it father, husband or son. Marriage was an inevitability; the class of elderly maiden ladies prevalent in Western society was unknown in China.

Because the population in China was so large and poverty widespread, and because girls were considered an expendable commodity, debt-stricken parents often sold their daughters to a wealthy family as a servant, or into prostitution. Gibson noted, "Since all girls ... must be provided with husbands, or else they are sold to infamy, it is sometimes thought best not to let them live at all." Female infanticide was practiced widely; girl babies were often drowned at birth, like kittens.

Those sold into prostitution were frequently children no older than twelve. They were, as Gibson says, "bought and sold, moved from place to place, and compelled to carry on their vile traffic for the benefit of their masters."

Because respectable wives were expected to tend the home fires, and also because few men could afford the additional $600 ship's passage to bring their wives with them, the great majority of San Francisco's Chinese female population in the nineteenth century were prostitutes: an estimated 90% in 1877. Some, like Ah Toy, the beautiful Chinese madame who arrived in San Francisco during the Gold Rush, came expressly to ply their trade. Others were kidnapped, tricked into signing false marriage contracts, or lured by the promises of rich husbands in the new country. Bought for $100 to $300 in China, "slave girls" sold for $300 to $600 in the United States.

Slave girls existed solely for the benefit of their owners; they were fed and clothed but never paid, and they were punished if their efforts were judged unsatisfactory. Says Gibson:

> In plying their vocation, if these girls fail to attract, or refuse to receive company and make money, the old mistress, whom they call "mother," beats and pounds them with sticks of fire-wood ... starves them, and torments them in every cruel way. ... Case after case of this kind has escaped ... and found refuge in the Methodist Mission House. They have sometimes come with arms, legs, and body bruised, swollen and sore, from the inhuman treatment received.

Some San Francisco missionaries, outraged by the atrocities they witnessed, made a special point of helping slave girls escape from their masters. One such missionary was Donaldina Cameron, who was no more than a girl herself when she began working at the Presbyterian Mission Home (later known as "920 Sacramento") in San Francisco in 1895. Although coming from an unlikely background for a religious zealot—her father was employed for many years by wealthy gambler-entrepreneur Lucky Baldwin—she soon made a name for herself rescuing, sheltering and educating Chinese slave girls and was credited with reducing the traffic by 50%. This line of work was not without its dangers; once one of the girls at "920" discovered some odd-looking bundles on the window ledges. These turned out to be sticks of dynamite, capable of destroying the building.

Donaldina Cameron and her fellow missionaries found that they had to contend with other forces when they attempted to interfere with the slave-girl trade. The Hip Yee Tong (ironically, "Temple of United Justice") controlled Chinese prostitution in San Francisco and specialized in protecting the property rights of slave owners. Their fee was $40 for each woman under their "protection." Often a man who had married a former slave girl was confronted by members of the Hip Yee Tong and given three alternatives: return the woman, reimburse her former owner for her full value, or be assassinated.

Attempts to prosecute slave owners or members of the Hip Yee Tong in court were generally unsuccessful; girls who had previously begged to be rescued were terrified at the thought of crossing their owners and refused to testify against them. Mrs. E. V. Robbins, in the *Overland Monthly* of January 1908, charged that some city officials, like the girls themselves, had been "bought":

> American lawyers and officials can be found who will, for a large fee, remand these poor girls to the slave den. Graft is a tame word for such cruelty.

Gibson expressed the opinion that

> There is no doubt that the municipal government could stop this traffic ... if it desired to do so. The trouble is, that a majority of those who compose our municipal government consider public prostitution a necessary evil, rather to be regulated than to be suppressed.

In the beginning, there were few women in Chinatown because of tradition and economic necessity. Later, immigration laws prevented them from joining their husbands. Although some men bought "second wives" or concubines to live with them, Chinatown was mainly a bachelor society. This situation is still reflected today in the disproportionately large ratio of men to women among the elderly.

"Crocker's Pets": Railroad Construction

[PICTURE PAGES 49–55]

On July 1, 1862, Congress passed the Pacific Railway Act, which chartered two railroad construction companies to build and operate a transcontinental railroad line. There was a political motive behind this Act: although the country was torn by civil war, the Western states had no declared loyalties. Congress hoped to insure Western loyalty to the Union by linking east to west by rail. It was agreed that the Central Pacific Railroad Company was to begin construction at Sacramento and work eastward, while the Union Pacific Railroad Company was to begin near Omaha and build westward. The proposed meeting point was at the California–Nevada border. The government had arranged for generous aid to the railroad companies: land grants along the railroad right-of-way, and cash loans per mile of track laid. The rate for this varied according to the terrain: $16,000 per mile for low-lying areas, $32,000 per mile in deserts and high plateaus, and $48,000 per mile in the mountainous regions.

Labor, however, proved to be a problem. Many men used railroad work only as a free means of transportation to the mining camps; once they had reached their destination, they left. Only one man in every ten stayed on the job longer than a week.

By this time, most of the Chinese had been driven out of the mines, and San Francisco was teeming with unemployed Chinese miners. In 1865, Charles Crocker, a former dry-goods merchant and one of the "Big Four" (with Mark Hopkins, Collis P. Huntington and Leland Stanford) who had backed Theodore Judah's fledgling Central Pacific Railroad Company, decided to capitalize on this potential labor pool by hiring Chinese to work on the railroad. The Chinese were thus given the epithet of "Crocker's Pets."

At first, the new workers were met with derision from their white co-workers, but Crocker cautioned that if the whites could not work with the Chinese he would fire them and hire all Chinese laborers. Historian Walton Bean stated:

> Labor unions in San Francisco protested, but as the railroad advanced into the mountains ... white workers lost all interest in jobs that required the performance of hard and dangerous labor under the conditions of labor in the Sierras.

The work was, indeed, "hard and dangerous." Using only hand tools—axes, picks, shovels, crowbars, sledgehammers—and blasting powder, the workers cut their way through the mountains. At times they were lowered in baskets down a sheer cliff face to blast out a path. Albert D. Richardson of the New York *Tribune*, who visited a C.P. construction site, described the scene as follows:

> The rugged mountains looked like stupendous anthills. They swarmed with Celestials, shoveling, wheeling, carting, drilling, and blasting rock and earth.

The Central Pacific kept no casualty records—possibly for fear of discouraging potential laborers—so it is not known how many Chinese perished in the Sierra Nevada. Estimates run from 500 to 1,000.

The Chinese laborers eventually earned the same salary as their white counterparts—$35 per month—but they, unlike the white workers, were required to provide their own food. This stipulation proved to be a blessing in disguise. The Chinese diet of rice, dried oysters, abalone, bamboo shoots, bean sprouts and poultry, all sent from San Francisco, was well balanced and protected them from the scurvy that afflicted many of the white workers. Because they drank only boiled liquids, they avoided dysentery.

The Chinese worked in crews of 12 to 20 men, each with its own cook and a headman who collected and distributed the wages. Tea carriers were designated to dispense hot tea to the workers, and barrels of warm water were made available at the end of each working day so that the men could bathe and wash their clothes. (Visitors to the camps were heard to remark that the other workers would do well to adopt the latter custom.) Each crew kept a few spare members so that even when someone fell ill, they had a full crew.

In 1866, encouraged by the progress of his laborers, C. P. Huntington persuaded Congress to change the Pacific Railway Act to allow each company to continue laying track until the two met. This small change made a great difference, for it made the Central Pacific and Union Pacific competitors rather than partners. It was a race to see which company would cover the most ground in the least amount of time.

The land faced by the two companies differed greatly: the Union Pacific had an easy time in the Great Plains, but the Central Pacific had to hack its way laboriously through the mountains. Even so, by 1868 the Central Pacific had managed to lay 140 miles of track to the Union Pacific's 500 miles. In 1868 12,000 of the 14,000 workers on the Central Pacific were Chinese, and it was in that year that 350 miles of track—close to Crocker's prediction of one mile per day—were laid.

The following year the two railroad companies passed each other in Utah and kept going. If Congress had not stepped in and declared Promontory Point, Utah, as the meeting point, there might someday have been two railroads running the length of the country, one hundred feet apart.

On April 29, 1869, a contest was held: the Central Pacific challenged the Union Pacific's record of eight miles in one day and readied a hand-picked crew of 848 Chinese, 41 teams of horses and carts and five trainloads of supplies. Between 7 A.M. and 7 P.M., "Crocker's Pets" set the world track-laying record— more than ten miles of track in 12 hours. In that time, they had laid 25,800 ties and 3,520 lengths of rail, and driven 55,000 spikes.

There were two completion ceremonies held, one in Promontory Point and one in Sacramento. Charles Crocker, speaking in Sacramento on May 8, 1869, said:

> In the midst of our rejoicing, I wish to call to mind that the early completion of this railroad we have built has been in a great measure due to that poor, destitute class of laborers called the Chinese—to the fidelity and industry they have shown—and the great amount of laborers of this land that have been employed upon this work.

Crocker's was the only speech that mentioned the importance of Chinese labor in the construction of the transcontinental railroad. Thus ended a major era in the history of the Chinese in America—with one short sentence.

The Chinese Must Go

[PICTURE PAGES 56–59]

The post-Civil War days at first seemed to herald better times for the Chinese in California. In 1867 Anson Burlingame, the former American minister to China, was appointed by the Chinese government to head a Chinese diplomatic mission to the United States. This mission drew up what came to be known as the Burlingame Treaty, which was ratified on November 23, 1869.

The Burlingame Treaty provided for, among other things, the mutual protection of citizens, the freedom of religion, the right to reside in either country, with all the privileges of favored nations. The Chinese were to have the right of admission to public schools in the United States and, conversely, American schools were to be established in China. There was to be an international exchange of currency and commerce.

Encouraged by the Burlingame Treaty, the Chinese came to the United States in even greater numbers; an average of about 15,000 immigrants per year arrived in the 1870's. Their sheer numbers began to alarm the American public; murmurs about the "yellow peril" grew. The docks of the Pacific Mail Steamship Company, which in 1867 had instituted a line of steamers between Chinese ports and San Francisco, became the setting for increasing abuse and violence.

The San Francisco *Times* of July 30, 1868, reported that a Chinese crab fisherman had been clubbed, robbed, branded with a hot iron and mutilated:

> There was apparently no other motive for this atrocity than the brutal instinct of the young ruffians who perpetrated it. Such boys are constantly hanging about our wharves, eager to glut their cruelty on any Chinaman who must pass.

California's Governor Newton Booth, in his inaugural address on December 8, 1871, warned:

> Mob violence is the most dangerous form in which the law can be violated. ... I trust that during my administration the spirit of lawless violence ... may never be exhibited. Should it be, there will be no exertion spared on the part of the executive to extend to all, from the humblest to the highest, the sovereign protection of the law and to visit the guilty with the punishment their crimes deserve.

Booth also referred to the Chinese as "a race notoriously defenseless" and to the unjust 1850 law which prevented them (as "Indians") from giving evidence in court. In 1872, possibly resulting from pressure in the governor's office, a California statute was passed which allowed Indians and Chinese to testify in court on the same basis as whites.

In the 1870's, however, the country was experiencing hard times. With the completion of the transcontinental railway came increased unemployment, as thousands of former railroad workers flooded the job market. The East Coast at that time was suffering from a postwar depression, and with the improved means of transportation, unemployed Easterners began pouring into California hoping to find work. In 1869 the population in the five Western states and territories affected by the railroad was 820,000; by 1870 it numbered over a million. The railroad also introduced competition from Eastern manufacturers and brought about a slump in Western profits.

Mining speculation also played a part in the spreading depression. The Comstock Lode, discovered in Nevada in 1857, was rich in silver, gold, copper and quartz. Stock gambling during the years 1874–1876 became a universal game; everyone, from the wealthiest magnate to the humblest clerk, owned mining stock. Says H. H. Bancroft:

> Seeing endless dividends in prospect, all classes were eager to possess shares in the great bonanza, which rose in value $10, $20, and $30 a day, and on one occasion as much as $100 at a single session of the board.

However, in 1876 the bottom fell out of the market—according to Bancroft, "from a variety of causes, chief among which was the natural reaction which inevitably follows undue inflation." Thousands of families were impoverished, and many businesses failed, resulting in greater unemployment.

1876 and 1877 were also years of drought. Damage to the grain crop and the loss of cattle amounted to deficits in the millions of dollars. Farmers and cattlemen alike were ruined.

Land monopoly created another problem. As was mentioned in the previous chapter, the Central Pacific held large land grants along the railroad right-of-way, and in addition, those who had arrived in the early days of the state still owned huge tracts of land. Small parcels were rarely sold, and then only for exorbitant sums. The poor, therefore, could not acquire cheap homes or earn their living as small farmers, and the employment of farm laborers was also hindered.

It was against this backdrop that Denis (also appears as Dennis) Kearney and the Workingmen's Party made their appearance. On July 23, 1877, a mass meeting of workers was held in San Francisco in the vacant lot near the new City Hall. Cheap Chinese labor, they charged, was responsible for the scarcity of work and low wages, for it was the Chinese who replaced Caucasian workers in the industrial force when they organized for higher pay and better working conditions. The speakers also denounced the moneyed and governing classes, nonenforcement of the eight-hour day, and land monopolies.

Offshoots from the mob—several hundred angry men—later roamed the city seeking Chinese to attack. Chinese men found in the streets were brutally beaten, Chinese prostitutes were dragged from their homes and abused. The mob wrecked a number of Chinese laundries in the area and burned one, at the corner of Turk and Leavenworth, to the ground.

San Francisco at that time was a wooden city which in its short history had already been destroyed by fire several times, and San Franciscans were alarmed by another threat of fire. The National Guard was called in. William T. Coleman, who had headed the 1856 Committee of Vigilance, organized a force of 1500 men—called the "pick-handle brigade" after their only weapon—who stood by to back up the militia. At the request of Governor William Irwin, three warships, the *Pensacola*, the *Lackawanna* and the *Monterey*, anchored off the San Francisco wharves, their guns trained on the Pacific Mail docks.

On the morning of July 25, six more Chinese laundries and stores were vandalized, and that afternoon 500 demonstrators grouped at the wharves of the Pacific Mail Steamship Company. Their original intent was to set fire to the docks, but, intimidated by the presence of the warships, they instead set fire to several lumberyards in the vicinity. The police, the National Guard and the pick-handle brigade held off the rioters in a shooting battle that lasted several hours and left many dead and wounded. Although the rioters were successfully dispersed, full order was not restored to the city for another three days.

Denis Kearney, one of the most aggressive foes of the Chinese in California, was a native of County Cork, Ireland, who went to sea as a cabin boy at the age of 11, and rose to first officer by the age of 21. Uneducated, but confident and accustomed to giving orders, Kearney arrived in San Francisco in 1868 aboard the clipper ship *Shooting Star*. He became a naturalized citizen in 1876.

Kearney operated a moderately successful draying business in San Francisco. However, he speculated heavily on mining stocks, which eventually plunged him into financial ruin. He then began giving soapbox lectures in empty lots, accusing the Chinese of conspiring with land and rail monopolies by accepting slave wages and undercutting white workingmen. He ended every speech with the slogan, "The Chinese must go!," which became his trademark. The San Francisco *Chronicle*, seeing an opportunity to boost its circulation, started reporting Kearney's speeches on a daily basis, and he soon became a hero to all "downtrodden workingmen."

On August 22, 1877, Kearney organized the Workingmen's Trade and Labor Union, which grew into the Workingmen's Party of California. Its objects were:

> To unite all poor and working men ... into one political party for the purpose of defending themselves against the dangerous encroachments of capital ... to rid the country of cheap Chinese labor as soon as possible by all means in our power, because it tends still more to degrade labor and aggrandize capital ... .

The charter went on:

> The party will then wait upon all who employ Chinese and ask for their discharge; and it will mark as public enemies those who refuse to comply with their request. ... It will encourage no riot or outrage, but it will not volunteer to repress or put down, or arrest, or prosecute the hungry and impatient who manifest their hatred of the Chinaman by a crusade against John or those who employ him.

The San Francisco branch of the Workingmen's Party met every Sunday afternoon on the vacant sandlot where the original mass meeting had been held, giving rise to the nicknames "sandlotters" and "Sandlot Party."

Although the charter of the Workingmen's Party denied that it encouraged "riot or outrage," Kearney himself called for violent action. "I advise everyone within the sound of my voice," he said, "to own a musket and a hundred rounds of ammunition." He also exhorted his followers to lynch the "Big Four" and destroy their property, dynamite Chinatown and burn the Pacific Mail docks. Kearney was arrested several times, but each time he was either acquitted or released on a technicality.

A wave of violence against the Chinese broke out all through the West, incited by Workingmen's Party members. (The San Francisco *Bulletin* said, "We ask why it is that these people [the Chinese] are beaten and maltreated at high noon on our streets and 'no arrests' invariably recorded.") In the 1878 elections in Alameda and Sacramento Counties, several of the Workingmen's Party candidates were elected.

Several ordinances directed at the Chinese were passed in San Francisco in the 1870's. The Cubic Air Ordinance of 1873 stated that any person found sleeping or lodging in a room or apartment containing less than 500 cubic feet of air for each person occupying it would be liable to a fine of $10 to $15 or imprisonment. The Chinese, of course, were the only ones who lived in such crowded conditions. On May 20, 1873, alone, 45 Chinese were arrested and incarcerated under this ordinance.

The Chinese community, however, saw a way to use this in their favor by overcrowding the county jail and at the same time receiving free food and housing. In answer, the San Francisco Board of Supervisors proposed the Queue Ordinance, which said that every male imprisoned in the county jail would immediately upon arrival have the hair of his head "cut or clipped to a uniform length of one inch from the scalp."

The Board of Supervisors also proposed a tax on all laundries not using animal-powered vehicles: $15 per quarter, as opposed to $3 per quarter for other laundries. Most Chinese laundrymen could not afford wagons and made their deliveries on foot, thus being liable to this tax.

The Cubic Air Ordinance was eventually overturned as being in excess of the Board's authority. The Queue Ordinance and the laundry tax were vetoed by San Francisco Mayor William Alvord, who wrote: "Minor offenses ... should not be punished by penalties which inflict disgrace upon the person of the offender." His decision was highly lauded by the American press:

> They have a brave man for Mayor of San Francisco [Chicago *Inter-Ocean*].

> All good citizens will sustain the Mayor in his rebuke of the bigoted Board of Supervisors [Oakland *Daily Transcript*].

> The action of Mayor Alvord meets the approval of the great majority of the public, including even those opposed to Chinese immigration, as the attempted legislation had taken the form of persecution [Boston *Journal*].

> When prejudice runs into persecution, as it seems to have done in California, it is time for honest and brave men, like Mayor Alvord, to put a check on it [New York *Herald*].

The Board of Supervisors, seeing that it lacked public backing, itself voted down the proposals on June 23, 1873.

Herbert Hill, in his article "Anti-Oriental Agitation and the Rise of Working-Class Racism" (*Society*, January/February 1973), observes that historically, radical or labor parties arise in the United States in times of high unemployment, when economic despair drives workers to seek new political solutions. With the reappearance of prosperity, these parties either disappear or merge with one of the two major political parties. This was the fate of the Workingmen's Party; its influence began to wane as the economy improved, and it was virtually powerless by the mid-1880's. The name of Denis Kearney was mentioned less and less frequently, and he gradually sank into obscurity.

The hatred of the 1870's, however, had set the wheels in motion, and many began calling for total exclusion of the Chinese.

The Development of Chinatown

[PICTURE PAGES 60–74]

In George Orwell's *Animal Farm*, the democratic slogan "All animals are created equal" is gradually changed by those in power to read "All animals are created equal, but some are more equal than others." So it was with legislative activity in the 1880's regarding Chinese immigration.

In 1880 the Burlingame Treaty was amended to allow the United States to regulate, limit or suspend, but not absolutely prohibit, the immigration of Chinese laborers. This, it was hoped by the anti-Chinese contingent, would open the way for indefinite "suspension."

On May 6, 1882, Congress passed the Chinese Exclusion Act, which suspended the immigration of Chinese laborers for ten years. The term "laborers" was extended to include skilled workers, such as doctors, journalists and clergymen, as well as unskilled workers; only those five classes specifically mentioned in the Burlingame Treaty (teachers, students, merchants, tourists and officials) were considered acceptable.

The Exclusion Act was aimed, in fact, at the annihilation of the Chinese population in the United States. In 1884 the Act was clarified to insure that the wives of Chinese laborers would also be denied entrance to the United States, thus condemning male Chinese laborers in this country to a life of bachelorhood. If married, they could not send for their wives; if single, they could not return to China to find a bride, for if they left the United States, they could never return, and anti-miscegenation laws in most states prevented them from marrying white women. (California's anti-miscegenation law, passed in 1872 to prevent white-black marriages, was amended in 1906 to include Mongolians and was not repealed until 1948.) Single Chinese women in San Francisco, as has been mentioned, were few and far between.

There were some native-born women, but the bulk of the female population in Chinatown was made up of merchants' wives and prostitutes. These factors explain the disproportionate number of elderly bachelors in Chinatown, even today.

The Scott Act of 1888 was a direct contravention of the Treaty of 1880 and thus unconstitutional. It expressly prohibited the immigration of Chinese laborers and permitted the entry of only the five specific classes. "Chinese" was defined as any member of the Chinese race, regardless of national origin. (Thus, a Frenchman holding Italian citizenship could enter under the Italian immigration quota, but a person of Chinese ancestry holding citizenship in another country was still considered Chinese.)

This was followed by the Geary Act of 1892, which extended all bills in force against the Chinese (i.e., the Exclusion Act) for another ten years. In 1902 it was again extended for ten years. The Chinese were the only people specifically named in legislation to be excluded from the United States.

As with any restrictive law, ways were found to circumvent these. Chinese born in the United States, and thus holding American citizenship, sometimes returned to China and stayed a sufficient time to record the birth of fictitious sons. Since offspring of American citizens were automatically granted citizenship, place of birth notwithstanding, they could later sell these "slots" to Chinese who wished to emigrate to the United States.

Most Chinese in California, however, were effectively isolated by the Exclusion Act and began to band together for protection and mutual benefit. They naturally constructed a society in their new environment which closely resembled that which they had known in the old country.

The basic unit in any Chinese community is the

family; thus, the basic organizations in Chinatown were the family associations. Made up of people who shared the same surname, and thus a common ancestor, the family associations looked after the welfare of their members and saw to their protection. Family associations at one time had great influence over their members; the weak were protected and the unruly held in check, disputes were settled between the members. The elders of the family associations were also responsible for caring for the sick and burying the dead.

District associations, the next level in the social structure, were made up of those originating from specific districts in Kwangtung (Canton) province. Only about 24 of the 90 Kwangtung districts were well represented among the Chinese in San Francisco, the others having only negligible representation. The district associations arbitrated differences between groups and businesses rather than individuals.

Sometimes, however, disputes arose between the district associations themselves. William Hoy, in *The Chinese Six Companies* (1942), comments:

> Naturally, since the courts and the majority of the Americans were plainly prejudiced against the Chinese, the latter did not bring their disputes to the American courts for settlement.

The Chinese Six Companies—officially, the Chinese Consolidated Benevolent Association—was formed to fill the need for an organization which could administer justice to all of the groups in Chinatown. Formed by the district associations then in existence—Kong Chow, Sam Yup, Sze Yap, Yeung Wo, Yan Wo and Ning Yeung—the organization has since been known as the Six Companies, even though new associations later joined and old ones broke away. In the 1890's it was actually composed of eight district associations.

The Chinese Six Companies was the official arbitrator for disputes arising amongst the district associations and other social groups. It also performed charitable functions such as caring for the aged and burying the dead. Even more than that, it was the mouthpiece for all California Chinese regarding problems and public affairs which affected their welfare. It was also given the power to initiate and promote programs on behalf of all the Chinese in California.

The so-called "fighting tongs" (*tong* simply means association or society) were formed by Chinese immigrants who had no strong family or district ties and thus had no association to depend upon for support or protection. These tongs, seeing the opportunity for financial gain and the accompanying power, gradually moved into illegal operations such as gambling, prostitution, narcotics, extortion and slavery. Each tong developed its own area of specialization. Charles Caldwell Dobie, in *San Francisco's Chinatown*, stated:

> The Hip Shing Tong controlled the gambling clubs; the Wa Ting Shans ... levied tribute on the brothels; the On Leong Society ... dealt in slave girls.

Disputes between tongs were not settled easily, as they lacked the conciliatory spirit found in other Chinese organizations, and a quarrel between members of two different tongs often erupted into bloody warfare between the tongs themselves.

Tong assassins were known as "hatchet men," after one of their favored weapons, or as "highbinders." The origin of the latter term has been traced to several different sources. Dobie says that Irish bandits in the 1820's belonged to an association called the "highbinders"; Arnold Genthe, the photographer best known for his Chinatown views, said that it came from the assassin's custom of binding his hair tightly on top of his head so that he could not be caught by the pigtail. John Manion, who headed the Police Department's Chinatown Squad from the 1920's on, stated that in the early nineteenth century, Irish bandits referred to a spree and drunk as a "high and bander." Whatever its origin, the word was synonymous with "gangster" and inspired terror in the hearts of most citizens.

The tongs enjoyed their period of greatest power from the 1880's until the 1920's. Eventually, all tong differences were settled by an arbitrating "Peace Society," and there has not been a tong war in half a century.

San Francisco's Chinatown around the time of the Exclusion Act was six blocks long, from California to Broadway, and two blocks wide, from Kearny to Stockton. Grant Avenue (then called Dupont Street) was then, as it is now, the main street, running through the center of Chinatown.

To the American visitor, Chinatown was a heady mixture of exotic sights, sounds and smells. The Rev. Otis Gibson wrote in the late 1870's:

> All day long, and often until late at night, the streets are crowded with Chinamen of all ages and sizes, and speaking various dialects, with shaven crown and neatly braided cue, sauntering lazily along, talking, visiting, trading, laughing, and scolding in the strangest and ... most discordant jargon.

Arnold Genthe, who came to San Francisco in 1895 from Germany, found himself drawn to Chinatown, which he considered a city within a city:

> The painted balconies were hung with windbells and flowered lanterns. Brocades and embroideries, bronzes and porcelains, carvings of jade and ivory, of coral and rose crystal, decorated the shop-windows. The wall-spaces between were bright with scarlet bulletins and gilt signs inscribed in the picturesque Chinese characters.

He described the aroma as

> the scent of sandalwood and exotic herbs from the drugstores, the sickly sweetness of opium smoke, the fumes of incense and roast pork, and the pungent odors from the sausages and raw meat.

The historian Zoeth Eldredge, less kind, wrote sarcastically that "when the Chinese quarter of San Francisco was being rebuilt after its purification by fire in 1906 ... the first thing reconstructed was the smell."

Every type of goods and services imaginable was available to the denizens of Chinatown. There were restaurants (it was said that around 1880, one could eat well at a Chinese restaurant for eight to ten dollars a month), laundries, stores selling dry goods, tea and herbs; butcher shops, vegetable stands, barber shops. By providing for the needs of their own community, Chinese merchants and tradesmen avoided competition with white businesses, and by patronizing Chinese-run stores, consumers took care of their own. Chinatown economically was a system of mutual support, of "Chinese for the Chinese."

Not that they were offered a choice; it was dangerous for them to venture past the boundaries of Chinatown. Young thugs in the Union Square area delighted in attacking any Chinese who strayed there. Only those with necessary and legitimate business, such as those working for a white household, left Chinatown. The Chinese would probably have gravitated to different parts of the city much sooner, had it not been for widespread prejudice in the larger community. Chinatown was a variation on Ben Franklin's statement during the American Revolution: "Gentlemen, we must all hang together, or assuredly we shall hang separately."

After Hours:
Mah-Jongg and Missionaries

[PICTURE PAGES 75–83]

Everyday life for the Chinese laborer was grim. Victor G. Nee and Brett de Bary Nee, who interviewed many of the old-timers in Chinatown for their book *Longtime Californ'*, say:

> The men remember the difficult search for employment, long hours of work, the small, crowded rooms where they lived with their cousins, two or three beds nailed one above the other, like shelves, onto the walls. They remember periods when the room was so crowded that even the beds had to be used in shifts by the men going back and forth to work.

Leisure hours were prized, and any form of entertainment—theater, gambling and other games, storytelling—was welcomed as a change from the monotony of the working day.

The first Chinese theater in San Francisco was opened on December 23, 1852, on Dupont (now Grant) near Green. The entire building, plus costumes and properties, was imported from China. The main area of a typical theater was nothing more than a large level floor filled with wooden benches, having a seating capacity of several hundred, with a separate gallery set aside for women. The stage itself was an elevated platform with entrance and exit doors at or near either wing.

The price of admission varied according to the time the ticket was purchased. At eight o'clock it was 50 cents, at ten o'clock it dropped to 25 cents, and at midnight it was a bargain 10 cents. The San Francisco *Chronicle* in the late 1870's remarked: "From an American standpoint, those who attend a Chinese theatre ought to receive a good salary paid in advance."

This, no doubt, referred to the fact that Chinese plays were extremely long; a single play often ran for days. There were seven different types of plots represented in Chinese plays: historical tragedy, comedy, platonic love, court, chivalry, persecution, and merit rewarded, and all were characterized by a stylized form of acting developed over centuries.

During the performance, vendors selling melon seeds, sweetmeats and fruit circulated among the audience. The audience themselves felt free to smoke, eat or move about while the play was in progress. Applause was not engaged in; only an occasional murmur of satisfaction was heard.

There were no women in the acting profession. All women's roles were taken by men who had been specially trained since childhood to imitate women's mannerisms, and who onstage wore small boots meant to resemble "lily feet." Chinese actors were well educated (they were required to have intelligence, wit, a good working knowledge of Chinese history and familiarity with court etiquette) and well paid, but they were not highly regarded. The starring system as we know it did not exist, and actors were prohibited from holding any government position. The latter prohibition also extended to the actors' children and their children's children.

Going to the theater filled the long evening hours and provided the men with the opportunity to socialize. In later years movie houses and girlie shows would serve the same purpose.

Gambling was also a popular leisure activity in Chinatown, at least until the 1920's, when the San Francisco police began cracking down on the gambling houses. Pai gow (dominoes), fan tan (a game in which the players each scoop a pile of beans from a bowl, remove four beans at a time, and bet on whether the remaining number is odd or even) and Mah-Jongg (an ancient Chinese game played with marked tiles) provided a spark of excitement and helped the men while away the hours. There were women, too, available for the right price, who could often be found participating in the games in the Mah-Jongg houses.

Storytelling was a respected art and an inexpensive source of entertainment. The men often visited each other's rooms for the stimulation of debate and gossip. Remarked one of the men interviewed by the Nees, "Everything, anything that comes along to our minds we made a story out of it."

Opium dens (or, as the San Francisco Municipal Report of 1884–1885 politely termed them, "opium resorts") did exist in Chinatown and provided a haven for those seeking a blissful form of escape. However, accounts of the opium dens, particularly in the early twentieth century, were highly sensationalized. Opium addiction was comparable to alcoholism in the white community: there were undeniably those who fell victim to it, but the greater part of the population could not afford the luxury.

Many Chinese in San Francisco became active in Christian churches, though traditionally the Chinese were uninterested in organized religion, considering religion to be an individual, not a social matter.

The Chinese view of religion omits the dichotomy of good and evil essential to Western religion: it is believed that all gods will treat men well under the proper circumstances. Chinese gods, after all, are as dependent upon the worshipper—for food, offerings, etc.—as he is on them. The Chinese have a saying: "One must not be blasphemous toward gods in whom one has no faith," the implication being that one never knows when an extra god may prove helpful in an emergency.

Francis Hsu, in *The Challenge of the American Dream*, explains the Chinese attitude in this fashion:

> The Chinese approach to temples and gods is not unlike our modern-day approach to stores. Some Americans prefer the Jewel supermarkets and others the Red Owl supermarkets. If they are dissatisfied with both, they may switch to National Tea stores. We have no reason to classify Chinese into Buddhists or Taoists any more than we can classify Americans into Jewellians or Red Owlists. ... Chinese temples have no records of memberships; they have no membership drives. They welcome all who want to come and pray; they never turn anyone away. ... For these reasons, the Chinese have not only shown no urge to proselytize but have had no history of religious persecution.

Of all Western religions, Catholicism comes closest to the traditional Chinese approach to religion. There are many saints and rituals, and priests who have the power of forgiveness; and purgatory (a finite punishment) is very close to the Chinese concept of hell. Two factors worked against widespread Chinese conversion to the Catholic faith. Because Catholics were also a minority in the United States, many Chinese were loath to join, thus becoming a member of yet another minority group. Also, Catholics from Ireland and southern Europe made up the bulk of the Workingmen's Party, which led attacks on the Chinese in California during the 1870's and 1880's. However, Old St. Mary's Church in San Francisco, founded in 1854, today possesses the largest Chinese membership of any church in the nation.

One of the main reasons for the success of Protestant and Catholic missions amongst the Chinese in San Francisco was the fact that they offered strong community-service programs rather than empty preaching. Dr. William Speer, the first Protestant minister to work with the Chinese in San Francisco, founded Presbyterian Mission in 1852. Also a physician who was fluent in Cantonese, Speer opened a free clinic at the mission and conducted adult English classes during the evenings. The missionaries also extended protection to the Chinese in the Kearney era and were vocal in their defense. In later years, under Margaret Culbertson and Donaldina Cameron, Presbyterian Mission became known for its rescues of Chinese slave girls and its care of delinquent girls.

Indeed, most of the Chinese Christian churches in San Francisco developed their own particular "specialties" as far as social service was concerned. The Methodists cared for Chinese orphans, met immigrants at the boat and cleared away red tape; the Catholics established a community recreation center, including a gymnasium and theater; the Baptists operated a boys' home; the Episcopalians ran a day school for children and a night school for adults. Often, Chinese schools, teaching children the language, history and culture of their forefathers, existed in conjunction with the Chinese Christian churches. The Hip Wo School, for instance, was sponsored by the Chinese Methodist Church and evolved into the most advanced Chinese school in the continental United States. Most of the churches also had one or two bilingual Chinese ministers on the staff.

The churches later served a useful purpose with the American-born Chinese, who, having no strong ties to family or district associations, still did not feel entirely comfortable with white social groups. Church functions provided the necessary feeling of fellowship, in a familiar, wholesome atmosphere.

All in all, whites who were curious to know what their faithful Chinese houseboy did on his day off would probably have been disappointed. Hours of talk with friends, attendance at a Chinese play or an adult-education class sound dull compared to the exotic pursuits—underground tunnels filled with opium dens and bagnios—in which the Chinese were purported to engage. Gim Chang, a retired rice merchant interviewed in *Longtime Californ'*, put it this way:

> When I was a boy, you know, I used to follow the older boys everywhere, and I knew all the dirty, secret places. When white people come to Chinatown looking for curiosities, I used to tag along behind the Chinese they took as guides, but I never saw an underground tunnel. Just mahjongg rooms in the basement.

New Era:
Death of Old Chinatown

[PICTURE PAGES 84–97]

On the morning of Wednesday, April 18, 1906, San Francisco was rocked by a huge tremor. Although lasting only 47 seconds, the 1906 earthquake was the greatest disaster in the city's history, still commemorated by annual observances today. Chimneys and cornices were shaken off buildings, cracks opened up in the streets, streetcar tracks buckled. Fires raged through the city—sparked by embers in cookstoves and fires kindled in defective chimneys—but the city water mains had burst during the earthquake, and there was no water. In desperation, buildings were dynamited to block the path of the fire. Many lost their lives; the city was filled with homeless refugees.

Chinatown, with its brightly colored banners and open-air markets, was leveled. The streets were filled with bricks and debris, and only a few walls and chimneys remained standing. Author Charles Keeler reported that by Wednesday evening, the Chinese, like others all over the city, were fleeing:

> Out of the narrow alleyways and streets they swarmed like processions of black ants. With bundles swung on poles across their shoulders, they retreated, their helpless little women in pantaloons following with the children, all passive and uncomplaining.

Some joined the scores of people waiting for the ferry to Oakland; others camped out with their fellow refugees in the city's parks and open areas.

There were those who mourned the death of Old Chinatown. Will Irwin, author of *Old Chinatown*, thought that the charm and beauty of Chinatown had been buried in the rubble, and Donaldina Cameron wrote:

> Heaps of sand and colored ashes mark the once densely populated, gaily painted, and proverbially wicked haunts of highbinders and slave dealers. ... The strange, mysterious old Chinatown is gone and never more will be."

There were those, however, who viewed the change not as an ending, but as a beginning. Louis J. Stellman, a former newspaper editor turned photographer, became one of the foremost chroniclers of new Chinatown, taking up where Arnold Genthe—who moved to New York in 1911—left off. Said Stellman: "A false impression prevails that Chinatown as it existed before the fire of 1906, is extinct. My pictures alone will disprove this."

Following the earthquake, there was a short-lived plan, proposed by former San Francisco mayor James D. Phelan, to relocate the Chinese quarter in Hunter's Point, far away from the city center. The San Francisco *Chronicle* of April 27, 1906, reported:

> Phelan objected strenuously to the concentration of the Chinese at the foot of Van Ness Avenue. Although the place was designed merely as a temporary camp, he said it would be extremely difficult to dislodge them if they once established themselves in that locality. ... He favored moving the Chinese at once to Hunter's Point. ...
>
> Gavin McNab did not favor the establishment of the permanent Chinatown at Hunter's Point, which, he pointed out, was just across the line in San Mateo county. He said San Francisco needed the property taxes and poll taxes of the Chinese more than ever before, and did not believe the city could afford to entertain an Oriental city just outside its boundaries.

Presumably motivated by the tax-paying power of the Chinese, the committee concerned with their housing voted to establish a temporary refugee camp for them in North Beach, at the foot of Van Ness

Avenue. Eventually, Chinatown was rebuilt in its former location.

Although catastrophic, the earthquake yielded an unexpected benefit for the Chinese in San Francisco. Because immigration records had been destroyed in the fire, many Chinese were able to claim citizenship. They were then free to send for their offspring in China, for legally all children of U.S. citizens were automatically citizens, regardless of their place of birth. The influx of "paper sons" helped to replenish Chinatown's youth and vigor. Hay Ming Lee, quoted in *Longtime Californ'*, noted:

> In the beginning my father came in as a laborer. But the 1906 earthquake came along and destroyed all those immigration things. So that was a big chance for a lot of Chinese. They forged themselves certificates saying they were born in this country, and then when the time came, they could go back to China and bring back four or five sons, just like that! They might make a little money off it, not much, but the main thing was to bring a son or nephew or a cousin in.

Journalism in Chinatown began to blossom during the first decade of the new century. In 1910 there were four Chinese dailies in San Francisco. The *Tai Tung Yat Po* (Chinese Free Press) was the most politically aggressive, advocating the overthrow of the Manchus and "China for the Chinese." The *Sai Gai Yat Bo* (Chinese World) was the most American, with a bilingual news staff and a California-born Chinese editor, Robert L. Park; the paper espoused the policies of the Reform Party, which called for deposing the Empress Dowager and seating the Emperor on the throne. The *Chung Sai Yat Po* (Chinese-Western Daily), whose editor, Ng Poon Chew, was one of the best-known English-speaking Chinese in the West, also had two Chinese associate editors with college degrees. *New Era* was a family-run enterprise established by the Yees, a large clan that included nearly all the Chinese laundrymen in San Francisco.

Lim Poon Lee, in the November 13, 1936, issue of *Chinese Digest*, wrote:

> The romance of the Chinese press on the Pacific Coast is very colorful, and behind each Chinese newspaper there was some interesting personality who had made history in one way or another. The Chinese people are intellectually inclined and responsive to new ideas—be they radical or conservative—and through the press, the Chinese leaders find their followers.

With more young people in Chinatown's ranks, education was naturally a concern, as the Chinese traditionally have a great respect for scholarship. Educational programs for the Chinese in San Francisco, however, were sparse.

The first school enrolling Chinese was founded in 1853 by a Mr. Moulton. Funded by wealthy Chinese and interested Americans, the school included pupils from 15 to 40 years old. In 1862 a Chinese school was established under the direction of the Board of Education, but it closed five years later because of managerial difficulties.

California State law at the time read:

> The governing body of the school district shall have power to ... establish separate schools for Indian children, and for children of Chinese or Mongolian descent. When such separate schools are established, Indian, Mongolian or Chinese children must not be admitted into other schools.

Because the implication was that those cities *not* having separate schools would have to admit Chinese children into public schools, the San Francisco Board of Education hastened to found a Chinese school. This school, begun in 1887, was located at 807 Stockton Street. Miss Rose Thayer was the first teacher, and the initial enrollment was 92 students.

By 1911, however, the facilities had fallen into disrepair. The Rev. John Hood Laughlin, writing in the *Overland Monthly* of May 1911, called the Chinese school building in San Francisco "a flimsy wooden shack, scarcely fit now to house the pupils." He pointed out that a large majority of the Chinese families who were driven to Oakland and other cities by the fire of 1906 had never returned, finding the school privileges in other locations somewhat better.

Because of discriminatory laws and prejudicial attitudes, many Chinese justly felt that educational and career opportunities were greater in China. Chinese-language schools were established here for the purpose of giving young men an education equivalent to that of their contemporaries in China. It was hoped that when they were older, they would be able to pass entrance examinations in China and complete their education there.

The first community-operated Chinese school in San Francisco (other private Chinese schools existed before this time) was the Ta Ch'ing Shu Yuan (the Ch'ing School), founded in 1884. School hours were engineered so that they began after normal public-school hours, or fell on weekends. Standards were high, for a young man's future sometimes hinged on the education he acquired there.

Until the Sino-Japanese War of the 1930's, it was a

common practice for American-born Chinese to enter school in China in their teens, marry there, and then return to the United States. Often, however, they found that they had been equipped with an insufficient amount of education in both English and Chinese.

The Chinese in San Francisco were instrumental in the foundation of the Chinese Republic. Excluded from participation in American economic, political and social life, the Chinese put their hopes in Sun Yat-sen and his followers: with the emergence of a new, strong China, they reasoned, treatment of overseas Chinese would surely improve.

Sun Yat-sen, born in China and educated in Hawaii, had dedicated himself to changing Chinese society. Between 1896 and 1911 he came to the United States six times, lecturing in Chinese communities across the country. San Francisco Chinese usually led those of other American cities in contributing to the revolution. Shirley Sun, in *Three Generations of Chinese—East and West*, comments: "The commitment of overseas Chinese to the Republican cause was an expression of their isolation and alienation from the American society."

In January of 1910, Sun Yat-sen established in San Francisco the T'ung Meng Hui (Together Sworn Society), which was the predecessor of the Chinese Nationalist Party. He also founded the *Young China Daily*, a newspaper still in operation today, as a means of communicating his views. In 1911, the T'ung Meng Hui merged with the Chee Kung Tong, an international secret society founded in 1848 and dedicated to the overthrow of the Manchus. This was a most profitable merger, as the Chee Kung Tong proved to be adept at collecting funds for Sun's revolution.

In October of 1911, the Manchu government fell. The Republic of China was founded, and Sun Yat-sen was chosen as its first president. This revolution was financed almost entirely by the contributions of overseas Chinese and was thus a source of pride to those who had believed in it and willingly given of their hard-earned money.

There was jubilation in Chinatown, with parades and speeches, as San Francisco's Chinese celebrated the end of almost three hundred years of tyranny. Following the lead of their countrymen in China, Chinese men in San Francisco cut off their queues, destroying the last vestige of their long subjugation. For the Chinese outside of China, the birth of the Republic had ushered in a new era of hope.

Second Generation

[PICTURE PAGES 98–103]

Chinatown in the 1920's had expanded, covering eight city blocks from Bush to Broadway, and three blocks from Kearny to Powell. It had been completely rebuilt after the earthquake and was again a bustling center of activity, its narrow streets overflowing with traffic, shoppers and tourists.

As in every poor immigrant community, illegal means of making money, such as narcotics trafficking, gambling and commercial sex, flourished. Six tongs—the Suey Sings, Bing Kongs, Suey Dons, Sen Suey Yings, Jung Yings and Hip Sings—emerged as powerful controllers of these operations and often engaged in combat when their territories collided. The "fighting tongs" maintained their power through fear: blackmail, threats and harassment. It was common practice for members of these tongs to walk out of stores openly with valuable merchandise, or to threaten or molest daughters, wives or other relatives of Chinatown merchants. These practices would stop only with the payment of a protection fee. Many respectable Chinese businessmen joined the tongs merely to gain immunity from the extortion and violence. Others solved the problem by moving to another city.

When Detective Sergeant John J. Manion was appointed to head the Chinatown Squad in March of 1921, the terrorism in Chinatown had reached a peak. Concerned about the violence and the dwindling population, Chinatown residents and merchants requested police protection, and the Chinese Six Companies pledged their cooperation. Jack Manion, a tough Irish cop, made it clear to the tongs that he would be a worthy opponent. During his first day on duty, two men were killed in tong warfare. Almost through sheer luck, the two men responsible were captured, and Manion prosecuted them for murder. One was hanged; the other died in San Quentin. It was the first time in San Francisco's history that tong killers had been caught, much less punished.

Big Pete, a gambler and member of the Suey Sing Tong for over 40 years, reminisced in *Longtime Californ'*:

> Do you remember Sergeant Manion? He was an inspector, and there was another inspector, Sergeant Dyer, and they were rough men. When they raided a place, anybody behind the table, if you don't get off that stool they'll bang the table against you. ... I mean they were cruel, they just didn't want anybody to gamble.

To be sure, Manion's tactics were unorthodox and would certainly not have been feasible today, but no one could deny that they were effective. In addition, the residents and businessmen of Chinatown supported Manion and his squad wholeheartedly, finding an occasional lapse of constitutionality preferable to terrorism.

Says one former member of the squad:

> We didn't need a warrant or anything. We just broke into the joint and frisked everything in there. ... If I wanted to go into a building and I thought something was wrong, I'd knock on the door and say, "Hoy man! Um cha!" (Open up! Policeman!). If there was no answer, I'd say, "Fa de la!" (Hurry up!). Well, if nothing happened then, I'd kick the door in. They'd all be in bed. I'd walk right through the joint. Nobody even hollered. Nobody said a word. You couldn't do that today. They'd sue.

In 1922, Manion called a meeting of the heads of the tongs and demanded an end to all illegal activities in Chinatown: "No more opium. No more gambling. No more tong wars or attempted bribes or shakedowns, and no more slave girls. Step out of line and you'll not only be arrested—you'll be deported."

Manion, originally appointed to the Chinatown Squad for a three-month term, ended up heading the squad until his retirement in 1946, and was considered the unofficial mayor of Chinatown. During his tenure, opium smuggling and slave-girl traffic disappeared (this last after Manion had put two slave dealers in San Quentin), and although lottery tickets were still sold in Chinatown, the actual drawings were held outside the city. By 1931, the *Police and Peace Officers' Journal* boasted that Chinatown was the safest spot in the city.

Between 1921 and 1926 alone, the population of Chinatown increased by 7,000 and, as the tongs' power was broken, this trend continued. Chinatown was well on its way to renewed growth and development.

Because immigration was almost impossible before the 1906 earthquake, Chinatown's second generation was not born until the 1920's. These American-born Chinese experienced the same problems faced by the children of other immigrants, only to a greater degree, because their physical appearance would not allow them to "pass" in the larger society. Not Chinese, yet not accepted fully as Americans, they were caught between two worlds. On one hand, they were pressed by their elders to conform to the Chinese values of respect and obedience, and on the other, they were encouraged by the American educational system to question the status quo and express their individuality.

Jade Snow Wong, author of *Fifth Chinese Daughter* and *No Chinese Stranger*, observed:

> The first generation of a racial group comes to America with a mature philosophy from their old world. They may not care about nor have to con-

sider the values they find in the new American world. But the second generation ... must decide about their own degree of acceptance of both old world and new. They must make a choice in defining their place within or between their two worlds.

Although by the 1920's the Chinese were no longer despised or seen as threats by the majority of white Americans, a certain amount of anti-Chinese sentiment was still apparent. William C. Smith, in the May 1926 issue of *Survey*, told of an American graduate of Stanford, then residing in Washington, D.C., who complained, "When I see American girls dancing with members of the Chinese and Japanese embassy, I can't stand it or understand how they do it."

The older generation of Chinese, concerned for their children's future, had emphasized Chinese studies and, whenever possible, had sent them back to China for several years of education. Always looking ahead, they tried to be prepared for the possibility that the Chinese in the United States would someday be expelled. Their children, however, realized that they were faced with a choice of Americanization or life in a ghetto, and did their best to adjust to two cultures and two sets of values.

This was not an easy task. Young Chinese-Americans attended high school faithfully to train themselves for white-collar jobs, only to find upon graduation that the job market was closed to them because of the color of their skin. Charles Caldwell Dobie, in *San Francisco's Chinatown*, commented caustically, "In spite of a lip-service affection which all San Franciscans indulge in when they speak of the Chinese, they will not open their working ranks to receive them."

The War Years

[PICTURE PAGES 104–119]

After World War I, Japan, under a militaristic, expansionist government, began to establish herself as the dominant power in Asia. The Japanese took over the strategic Chinese province of Shantung and presented China with the "21 Demands," which, in effect, demanded the unconditional surrender of China's sovereignty. The new Republic refused, and animosities broke out betwen the two nations, who were historical enemies.

In 1921 Japan seized the Manchurian provinces in the northeast of China, and by 1937 full-scale warfare had erupted. The Kuomintang (Chinese Nationalist Party) and its internal foe, the Chinese Communist Party, called a reluctant truce and united forces against Japan.

In America, missionary groups began to boycott Japanese goods ("Silk Stockings Kill Chinese") and to protest the shipment of arms and supplies to Japan. They told of the heroism of the Chinese and the brutality of the Japanese. Public sentiment against the Japanese began to grow and, conversely, so did support for the Chinese.

Again, overseas Chinese rallied to the cause. In 1938, 10,000 San Francisco Chinese and their supporters staged a demonstration at the docks to protest the shipment of scrap iron to Japan, carrying signs reading "Scrap Iron Becomes Bullets." Organizations such as the Save China Youth Association and the Chinese Workers Mutual Aid Association sprang up to raise money for the Chinese Republic. Worldwide, overseas Chinese bought over $500 million in war bonds to aid the war effort. At the suggestion of Madame Chiang Kai-shek, a special infantry division of Chinese-Americans was formed, and many men from San Francisco's Chinatown enlisted to fight in China.

On December 7, 1941, Japanese planes attacked the American fleet at Pearl Harbor, and the United States entered the war. This was a turning point for Chinese-Americans, for it marked their first major entrance into the mainstream of American society. For the first time, American-born Chinese men were able to compete on an equal basis with white males: they wore the same uniform, fought under the same flag and performed an equally valuable function. Journalist Charlie Leong said:

> To men of my generation, World War II was the most important historic event of our times. For the first time we felt we could make it in American society. [We] were part of the great patriotic United States war machine out to do battle with the enemy.

Even those Chinese who were not American-born and did not speak English were eager to be included in the war effort. In 1943 an aircraft subassembly plant, sponsored by China Aircraft, Inc., and supported by the Army Material Command, was opened in California. Staffed almost entirely by Chinese, the plant turned out parts for the Douglas A-20 Havoc light bomber. Additionally, the program tapped the Chinese-speaking labor pool and boosted the morale of Chinese workers, who, because of language difficulties, had not previously been able to find work in war plants.

1943 was important for the Chinese in America. That year, spurred by public sentiment in favor of America's Chinese allies, President Roosevelt asked Congress to repeal the Chinese Exclusion Act. The repeal was signed into law on December 17. Besides abolishing all existing legislation pertaining to the exclusion of the Chinese, it also restored the right of naturalization to Chinese entering the United States legally. That same year, Madame Chiang Kai-shek had made a highly successful tour of the United States to plead for aid to China. The fiery rhetoric of the beautiful Madame Chiang, a graduate of Wellesley College, greatly increased American sympathy to the Chinese cause. Says Shirley Sun, "Never before and never again have the Chinese stood on such a high pedestal."

This adulation was short-lived, for disillusionment with the corruption in Chiang's government quickly followed, and soon after World War II, China became not a single entity but two warring factions, as civil war broke out between the Nationalist and Communist parties.

Although heavily supported by American military aid, Chiang's armies were defeated by Mao Tse-tung's well-trained Communist troops. In 1949 the Communists gained control of China, founding the People's Republic of China, while the Nationalists fled to Taiwan.

This was a landmark in the lives of first-generation Chinese in the United States. Unable to identify with either the Nationalist or the Communist governments or to visit their ancestral homeland, they were forced to focus their attention on life in America.

In the late 1940's there was a further loosening of restrictive statutes. The War Brides Act of 1946, an amendment to the exclusion repeal, permitted wives of Chinese-American men to enter the United States as non-quota immigrants. Eight thousand women entered the country under this act before it expired at the end of 1949. In San Francisco in 1947, the ordinance which had prohibited Chinese from buying homes outside of Chinatown was lifted, thus prompting a move to the suburbs—mainly the lower middle-class Sunset and Richmond districts. In 1948 the California legislature struck down the state's anti-miscegenation law, which had prevented Oriental-Caucasian intermarriage since 1906.

Despite these legislative votes of confidence, racial discrimination lingered on. Since the 1930's, Chinese students had entered the local institutions of higher education—San Francisco State College, City College, University of California at Berkeley, Mills College and Stanford University—without much difficulty. They found, however, that their career opportunities, even with a college degree, were severely limited. Sam Lee, who headed the Chinatown branch of the California State Employment Service in the 1940's, stated:

> They are just as smart as boys and girls with white skin. But who wants to employ a Chinese college graduate? ... If you are a chemist, you almost have to win the Nobel prize before you can get a job in an American lab.

He gave several jarring examples: a Ph.D. in architecture from UC-Berkeley who worked in a barbecue stand, an electrical enginer who sold liquor in Chinatown, a holder of a master's degree in journalism who made his living as chauffeur to a wealthy white woman.

Having tasted of equality, however briefly, the second generation found their homecoming a bitter one.

Postwar to the Present

[PICTURE PAGES 120–131]

The 1950's saw the decline of Chinatowns in the United States. The Exclusion Act had been repealed; Chinese immigrants were now allowed to become citizens and own property outside of Chinatown. Acculturation and assimilation took place more rapidly as the Chinese population was distributed more evenly throughout the white community.

With the postwar baby boom, the second generation, the Chinese-American, gave way to the third, which could be more accurately described as "American Chinese." These children spoke English as their first language; their knowledge of Chinese customs and language was negligible. This effect was magnified by the change in the Chinese family unit. Because both parents often worked, the family structure was not as tight as before. Children were less influenced by the family and the Chinese model of unquestioning obedience and more by the American ideas of independence and individuality.

Prejudice in the white community was not as blatant as in previous years—American-educated Chinese at least were able to find white-collar jobs—but it remained. "We get steady positions as professional workers," said an engineer, "with a steady, middle-class income. We'll get a slight promotion, but after that the subtle discrimination comes in." Although Chinese were often hired in great numbers to work in such fields as computer programming and accounting, they were kept from advancing to the decision-making level.

White America, for its part, created a myth around the Chinese, whom they held up to other ethnic groups as a "success story." The Chinese were described in numerous articles in the 1950's as clean, industrious and uncomplaining, with no juvenile delinquency because of close family ties. Healthy, happy suburban families were stressed; poor housing,

unemployment and discriminatory hiring practices were ignored, as were the street gangs that were then beginning to form.

There were many among the Chinese community who came to believe in these myths. In the September 1955 issue of *American Magazine*, Edmond Gong, the American-born son of Chinese parents and a student at Harvard Law School, stated that he felt American and had never experienced any identity crises or racial prejudice. He went on to say:

> While a girl of Chinese ancestry might be the best choice for me, I have never met or seen such a girl who really attracted me. ... My ideal of grace and beauty runs more to someone like Grace Kelly or Ava Gardner.

Chinese Americans during the 1950's were not noted for their vocal participation in American politics and were particularly silent during the McCarthy witch-hunts and the Korean War. Memories of the concentration camps for Japanese in America during the Second World War were still fresh, and many Chinese feared the same fate. Their fears were not unwarranted. As late as 1969, FBI Director J. Edgar Hoover testified that Chinese Communists were still the number-one enemy of the United States and that all Chinese-Americans were potential spies because of their ethnic ties.

In the 1960's, immigration laws were eased further. Since Mao Tse-tung had taken control of China, there had been a steady stream of immigrants into Hong Kong. In 1962, John F. Kennedy signed a law that permitted these refugees entry into the United States, and in 1965, Lyndon Baines Johnson approved a law that abolished national-origins quotas over a three-year period. The total annual quota for all countries was set at 170,000, and by 1968 all immigrants were to be processed in order of application. During the 1960's, 30,000 Chinese entered San Francisco.

This new wave of immigration renewed Chinatown's growth, but it also posed additional problems. By 1970 there were well over 40,000 people living in the 42 blocks that comprised Chinatown, a density rate of 885.1 persons per acre—over ten times the San Francisco city average. Living conditions were crowded and often below standard, working conditions were bad, and the rate of tuberculosis was double that of San Francisco as a whole.

Approximately 50% of the population in Chinatown was under the age of 21. Most of these were unskilled young immigrants from Hong Kong, Macao and Taiwan with few family ties. Lacking an education, a knowledge of English or the patronage of a clan association, they were unable to find jobs. Those available to them were scarce and ill-paying: an average of 60¢ per hour in the garment factories and $1.20 per hour in the restaurants.

The first FOB ("fresh off the boat") gang was formed in 1968. The Wah Ching (China Youth) was to be a combination social club and job corps. However, when their attempts to enlist the aid of the Chinatown establishment in placing their members for jobs failed, the youths became embittered and turned to robbery and extortion as a more reliable means of making money. In 1972 a rival gang, the Chung Chin Yee (the Joe Fong Gang or Joe Boys) was formed, and territorial battles between the two groups developed. There were 430 juvenile arrests in San Francisco in 1972, compared to 85 in 1964, and between 1970 and 1973 there were 13 gang-related killings.

Certainly young Chinese are leaving Chinatown at the rate of 15,000 a year, abandoning it to recent immigrants, the old and the unemployed.

Even so, the prospects for Chinatown are bright. The ethnic-pride movements of the '60's and '70's have made Chinese in San Francisco conscious of their unique heritage—Chinese tradition rooted in American soil—and proud of their history. Organizations such as the Chinese Historical Society of America, the Asian-American Theater, Northeast Medical Services (NEMS) and Combined Asian Research Project (CARP) have been formed for the purpose of promoting awareness of Chinese-American history and bettering existing social conditions. Groups such as these are seeking out old-timers to record their stories, so that future generations will know "the way it was"; they are fighting for low-cost housing, better health care and bilingual education for Chinatown's residents; they are encouraging contemporary Asian-American art and literature and teaching new arrivals the English and job skills necessary to live in an American society.

The idea of Chinese mutual support is not new; it helped the Chinese in California through the turbulent mining days and the violent Kearney era, and it is one which carries validity even today. Survival for any ethnic group must come from within; we as Chinese-Americans must see that the old ways are not lost, that a sense of pride in their heritage is instilled in our children, that our people receive all the rights guaranteed to them as Americans. Only in this way—by using the best of the past and the present—can we fully enjoy the richness of our two cultures.

Early Immigration and Mining

Chinese emigrants waiting to board ship for *Gum San* (Land of the Golden Mountain). The voyage from China to San Francisco took two months, on the average. It was a rough passage; the Chinese crowded into the dark holds often suffered from abuse and malnutrition. Many did not reach California alive. Wood engraving from a contemporary magazine. (*California Historical Society*.)

San Franc. in '4[...]

Opposite, top: San Francisco, as seen in this lithograph of ca. 1847, was a sleepy village of dirt paths and a few permanent structures. This was to change radically in the next year, as gold was discovered at Sutter's Mill and thousands of would-be miners from all over the world arrived to seek their fortunes. (*California Historical Society.*) Opposite, bottom: "A very large party of Celestials attracted considerable attention yesterday evening ... on their way to the southern mines. They numbered about fifty, each one carrying a pole, to which was attached large rolls of matting, mining tools, and provisions ... They ap-

peared to be in excellent spirits and in great hopes of success" (*Alta California*, 1852). This wood engraving of "A Road Scene in California" appeared in the *Wide West*, a short-lived newspaper which provided its readers with excellent pictorial representations of life in the West. (*California Historical Society.*) Above: San Francisco in 1849 was a city of tents and temporary structures, host to a large population of transients. San Francisco's harbor was crowded with seagoing vessels, many of which were abandoned when their crews jumped ship to look for gold. (*California Historical Society.*)

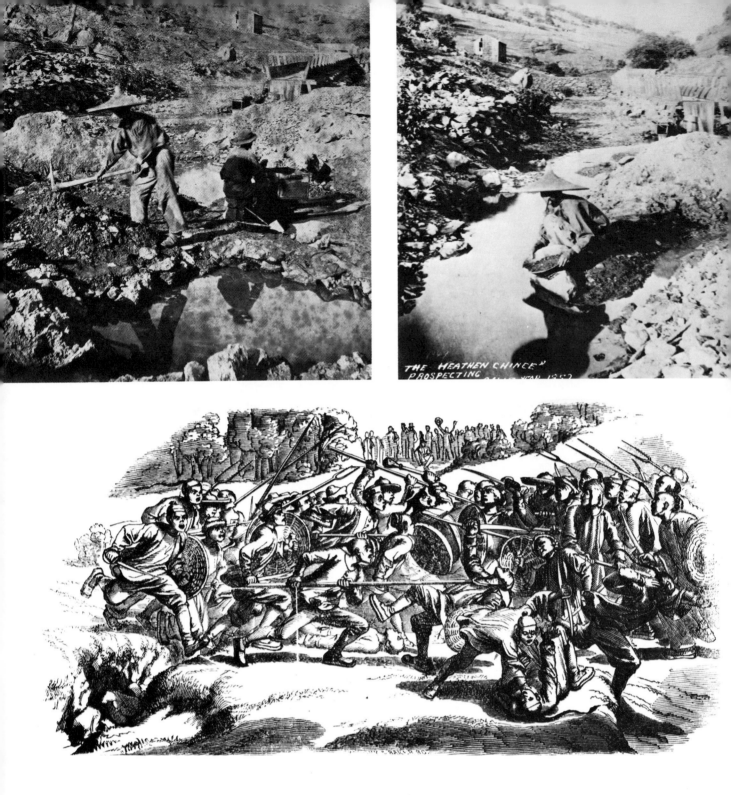

Top, left: The Chinese in their loose blue cotton clothing and broad-brimmed hats soon became an everyday sight in the mines. They operated on worked-over claims and unpromising sites to avoid competition with white miners, a situation which they had found could be dangerous. (*California Historical Society.*) **Top, right:** Chinese miners used the most primitive of mining tools—the pan and rocker—which had the advantage of low maintenance and portability. This photograph was taken in 1852. Note the photographer's notation: "the heathen Chinee." (*California Historical Society.*) **Bottom:** "A Chinese Battle in California," from the *Wide West*, depicting a battle which took place in Weaverville, near Five Cent Gulch, in June of 1854 between rival tongs (fraternal organizations) of Chinese miners. The battle was prepared for several weeks in advance; fashioning weapons ordered by both factions, one local blacksmith supposedly made $1500 in profits. An estimated 575 Chinese were involved, and 11 were killed, as was an American who fired into the group. No reason for the battle was ever disclosed, but presumably the dispute was settled to everyone's satisfaction, for the two tongs never fought again. (*California Historical Society.*)

Early Days in San Francisco

Portsmouth Square, 1850 (then called the Plaza), site of the first meetings in San Francisco to which the Chinese were invited. Several hundred of the "China boys" turned out for the ceremonies, and their subsequent letter of thanks to the people of San Francisco was printed in the *Alta California*. (*California Historical Society*.)

Top: Washerwoman's Lagoon, San Francisco, 1856. Located some two miles west of the then city limits, Washerwoman's Lagoon served as the largest freshwater "laundry" in the city. The building in the foreground is the Loveland residence, at what is now the intersection of Gough and Filbert Streets. (*California Historical Society.*) **Bottom:** Illustration from the *Wide West* entitled "A Chinese Wash-House." The Chinese entered the laundry business at a time when there was a shortage of women in California and laundry was often sent as far as Honolulu and Canton. Opening a laundry required little capital and only a few simple pieces of equipment. The first Chinese wash house was established near Portsmouth Square. (*California Historical Society.*)

Top: A Chinese laundryman of a later period poses proudly on a San Francisco street corner. Because Chinese laundries picked up and delivered, the actual location of the business was unimportant, and it was possible to keep overhead low. Originally, laundry was transported on a bamboo pole with baskets suspended on each end, but during the anti-Chinese movement of the 1870's, an ordinance was enacted prohibiting the use of poles. (*Gabriel Moulin Studios.*) **Bottom:** The rough Chinese cafés of the Gold Rush days, which catered to homesick Chinese and white miners weary of bread and potatoes, grew into the second most prevalent occupation of the Chinese in America. This photograph of an elegant restaurant in San Francisco's Chinatown was taken around 1890. (*Southern Pacific Transportation Company.*)

Above: Deck view of a Chinese fishing junk on San Francisco Bay. Many Chinese turned to the fishing industry in the 1850's after the racial situation in the mines began to deteriorate. The fish were cut up, dried and sold in town or to Chinese bound on journeys. (*San Francisco Maritime Museum.*) **Opposite, top:** Shrimp junk, San Francisco Bay. A visitor to a fishing camp on the Sacramento River in 1873 described similar vessels as being "strongly built, but narrow and pointed at both ends. ... Two of the three large boats had one mast, and the other one had two masts ... with Chinese sails. The whole air and look of these crafts was decidedly foreign." (*San Francisco Maritime Museum.*) **Opposite, bottom:** A group of Chinese at McNear's Beach in Marin County, north of San Francisco, 1906. There were Chinese shrimp camps located at nearby Point San Quentin and Point San Pedro. (*San Francisco Maritime Museum.*)

Opposite, top, left: Using fine-mesh nets imported from China, Chinese shrimp fishermen made California one of the greatest shrimp-producing states in the nation. Protests from Greek, Dalmatian and Italian fishermen, however, resulted in an 1870's law regulating the size of mesh used. (*Bancroft Library.*) **Opposite, top, right:** Fishermen drying shrimp and squid along San Francisco Bay, ca. 1895. In 1897 there were an estimated 26 shrimp camps operated by Chinese on San Francisco Bay. Each camp had its own "territory" in the shrimp beds, which was respected by the other camps in the area. (*Thomas W. Chinn Collection.*) **Opposite, bottom:** Chinese whalers, possibly near Monterey. There was a large Chinese colony in Monterey, one of the principal fishing centers on the West Coast. Residents of the village also gathered seaweed from the shores of the Monterey Peninsula, to be dried and sold. (*California Historical Society.*) **Above:** Photograph taken ca. 1868 by Eadweard Muybridge—originally a stereographic view—entitled "Point Reyes—The 'Heathen Chinee' abaloni merchant at Drake's Bay." Abalone were sold for the meat and the shells, which were used for inlay work in China and for jewelry and ornamentation in Europe and the eastern United States. (*California Historical Society.*)

Opposite, top: Chinese workers loading rice bundles onto a salmon packet bound for Alaska on April 12, 1906, six days before the great earthquake and fire. Chinese were not allowed to participate in the salmon fishing industry but were employed in canneries in the Northwest, British Columbia and Alaska almost exclusively. It is no coincidence that the machine which later replaced cannery workers was known as an "Iron Chink." (*San Francisco Maritime Museum.*) Opposite, bottom: "The Vegetable Peddler," by Arnold Genthe, ca. 1900. A housewife in Chinatown looks over the day's produce. Chinese truck gardeners cultivated their crops outside the city limits and were a familiar sight with their bamboo poles and baskets. (*California Historical Society.*) Above: Chinese vegetable gardens at Union and Pierce Streets, San Francisco, ca. 1885. Today this is a fashionable area of boutiques and restaurants. (*California Historical Society.*)

Opposite, top: A vegetable peddler, selling his wares door-to-door, almost dwarfed by his baskets. The white-coated man on the left, his queue neatly wound around his head, is probably a cook purchasing fresh vegetables for his employer's household. (*California Historical Society.*) **Opposite, bottom:** Rag gatherer, San Francisco. This service, performed for the paper industry, was dominated by the Chinese. (*Society of California Pioneers.*) **This page, top:** Chinese servant in the garden, possibly in Berkeley. The Chinese were much prized as cooks and domestic help and received wages which were up to twice as high as the average rate for household servants. (*Graves Collection, Bancroft Library.*) **This page, bottom:** "Charlie my cook while at Belvedere, 1897." Well-to-do families kept summer homes on Belvedere Island in Marin County. Working for a wealthy Caucasian was once a status symbol among the Chinese. (*Oakland Museum.*)

Top: Garment worker, San Francisco, ca. 1880. At that time there were an estimated 2,000 Chinese in the clothing manufacturing industry; approximately 80% of all shirtmakers in San Francisco were Chinese. The industry then was predominantly male and controlled by Chinese trade guilds which regulated hours, wages and working conditions—quite different from today's garment factories in Chinatown, which are almost exclusively staffed by women and are non-unionized. (*Society of California Pioneers.*) **Bottom:** Chinese laborer at the Selby Smelting and Lead Company, San Francisco. Although the Chinese in later years were accused of lowering wages, the average wage in San Francisco was higher than in the Eastern states. An iron molder during the years 1870–1890, doing a job similar to the man in the photograph, made between $3.40 and $3.70 a day. (*California Historical Society.*)

Chinese Women

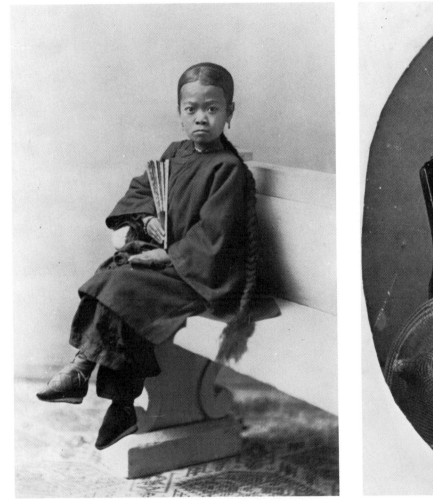

Left: Foot-binding was a mark of high class; women with "lily feet" were considered better marriage prospects. Binding began between the ages of three and eight years. The toes were turned under, the foot pulled straight with the leg, and a long narrow cloth bandage wound tightly around the foot from the toes to the ankle. This intensely painful process checked the growth of the foot permanently; women with bound feet could stand or walk only with difficulty. Bound feet, however, were rare in San Francisco. Girls of the laboring classes and those destined for prostitution did not have bound feet, and it was from one or the other of these that most Chinese women in San Francisco came. Photo by Isaiah West Taber, San Francisco (1830–1912). (*Bancroft Library*.) **Right:** Portrait of a typical Chinese woman in *Gum San*, possibly a servant. Note the unbound feet. (*California Historical Society*.)

Above: "Slave Girl in Holiday Attire," ca. 1900, by Arnold Genthe. Slave girls were prostitutes whose activities profited their owners. Bought in China for $100 to $300, they were sold in the United States for two and three times that amount. (*California Historical Society.*) **Opposite, top:** Donaldina Cameron (known as *Lo Mo*, which can be roughly translated as "The Mother") and a group of her girls at the Presbyterian Mission Home at 920 Sacramento, San Francisco. For decades Miss Cameron fought the slave-girl trade, rescuing hundreds of girls from brothel slavery. (*Society of California Pioneers.*) **Opposite, bottom:** Chinese women in San Francisco before the turn of the century. Photographs of unescorted women outside the boundaries of Chinatown were rare during this time; respectable women stayed close to home. Only once every seven years, on the Festival of the Good Lady, were Chinese women allowed to walk the streets freely, like men. (*Southern Pacific Transportation Company.*)

A group—wearing the silk robes and embroidered slippers that signify a holiday or special occasion—in Golden Gate Park in the 1890's. Chinese women spent their entire lives serving a man, be it father, husband or son. (*Bancroft Library.*)

"Crocker's Pets": Railroad Construction

Charles Crocker, 1822–1888, one of the "Big Four" of the Central Pacific Railroad Company, who first hired the Chinese to work on the transcontinental railroad. His stubborn support of the Chinese workers, over the protests of organized labor, earned the Chinese the sobriquet of "Crocker's Pets." (*California Historical Society.*)

Above: This photograph was taken by Alfred A. Hart, the official Central Pacific photographer, at Heath's Ravine, 82 miles from the start of the Central Pacific line in Sacramento. The Chinese laborers pictured are filling in the roadbed to the higher level; they worked on two or more levels at once to speed construction. (*Southern Pacific Transportation Company.*) **Opposite, top:** Tea carrier, east portal of Tunnel No. 8, 105 miles from Sacramento. Each Chinese work crew had its own cook and appointed helpers to carry hot tea to the workers. Because they drank only boiled liquids, the Chinese seldom contracted the dysentery that plagued Caucasian railroad workers. A. A. Hart photograph. (*Southern Pacific Transportation Company.*) **Opposite, bottom:** View of the headquarters train, horse camp and Chinese camp on the Humboldt plains of Nevada during the last year of construction, 1868. In that year, the Central Pacific laid 350 miles of track, close to Crocker's prediction that his crews would do "one mile per day." A. A. Hart photograph. (*Southern Pacific Transportation Company.*)

Railway workers at Secrettown trestle, in the Sierra Nevada, east of Gold Run. Note the wheelbarrows and one-horse dump carts used. Dynamite had by then been invented, but was not yet in general use; laborers on the Central Pacific used hand tools such as picks, shovels and axes, and black blasting powder. (*Southern Pacific Transportation Company.*)

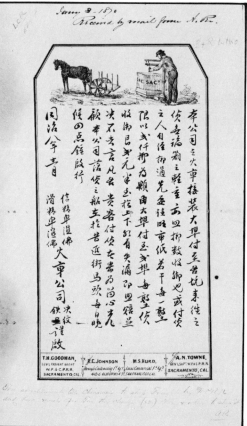

Opposite, top: Site of the track-laying contest held near Promontory Point, Utah, on April 28, 1869. The Central Pacific had challenged the Union Pacific record of eight miles in one day. Using a hand-picked crew of 848 Chinese, the Central Pacific laid ten miles of track in 12 hours. Photo taken 1927. (*Southern Pacific Transportation Company.*) **Opposite, bottom:** This advertisement was written in a form of Chinese shorthand called "grass writing"—some of the characters are no longer in use today. The text reads: "Our Company's trains will accept goods for shipment to and from San Francisco, and regardless of the weight of the crates, the freight will be weighted according to pounds. If the sender weighs the goods himself, he must first indicate the weight on the voucher. One ton equals 2,000 pounds. We charge $2.50 to ship one ton of freight from San Francisco to Sacramento. Goods lost during shipment will be reimbursed. This we guarantee [literally, "We will absolutely not eat our words"]. We hope all of our customers will patronize us. Our ships will load at the Second Street wharf and will sail each afternoon at 4 P.M. [signed] Hurd and Goodman of the Central Pacific and Western Railroad Company." The ad is dated "The eleventh month of the eighth year of T'ung Chih." T'ung Chih, an emperor of the Ch'ing Dynasty, came to the throne in 1862. The ad, therefore, was written in November of 1869. (*California Historical Society.*) **Above:** Completion of the transcontinental railway, Promontory Point, May 10, 1869. In 1863 the Central Pacific had begun construction in Sacramento, working eastward, and the Union Pacific had begun in Omaha, working westward. Although the original meeting point had been set as the California–Nevada border, the Central Pacific made better progress than had been expected, and the meeting point was left open. Chinese laborers made up a good 86% of the Central Pacific work force, but their role was largely ignored during the completion ceremonies. (*Bancroft Library.*)

The Chinese Must Go

Left: Chun Lan Pin, first Chinese ambassador to the United States, photographed by Bradley & Rulofson, San Francisco, ca. 1871. The Burlingame Treaty, signed by the United States and China in 1869, guaranteed the mutual protection of citizens, freedom of religion and the right to reside in either country, with all the privileges of favored nations, including the right to attend public schools. (*California Historical Society*.) **Right:** Dennis Kearney, an Irish drayman who was himself a new-comer to the United States, was the founder of the anti-Chinese Workingmen's Party of California and the creator of the slogan, "The Chinese must go!" He enjoyed a brief period of power during the late 1870's, during which time he stated, "I hope I will be assassinated, for the success of the movement depends upon that." There were those of his opponents who fervently hoped that his dreams would be realized. (*California Historical Society*.)

THE TABLES TURNED
YOU SABE HIM ? KEALNEY MUST GO !

To my Friend C.H.Harris Carl Pretzel "Der leedle Wanderer"
THE HEATHEN CHINEE
And he went for that Heathen Chinee

SONG & CHORUS

WORDS by BRET HARTE
MUSIC by CHAS. TOWNER.

Published by S. BRAINARD'S SONS, Cleveland.
107

Top: This cartoon appeared in a San Francisco paper around 1878, during one of Kearney's brief stays in the "House of Correction." Although Kearney was arrested several times, he was always acquitted or released on a technicality. (*California Historical Society.*) **Bottom:** Because of Chinese laborers' willingness to work for any wage, however meager, they were accused of cheating white workingmen out of jobs and lowering the pay scale. However, as Mary Roberts Coolidge pointed out in *Chinese Immigration* (1909), Chinese labor never remained cheap for long—between 1882 and 1909, Chinese wages increased faster than those of white workers—and their ambition inevitably moved them out of the laboring classes into small businesses. The portion of Bret Harte's poem illustrated in the smaller inset on this song cover reads: "Then I looked up to Nye,/And he gazed upon me,/And he rose with a sigh,/And said, 'Can this be?'/We are ruined by Chinese cheap labor,'/And he went for that heathen Chinee." (*J. S. Holliday Collection.*)

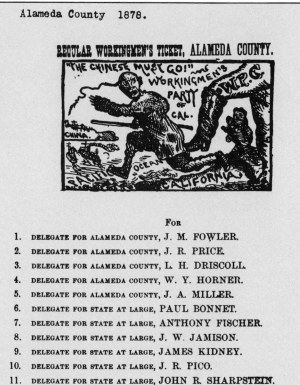

Opposite: The Pacific Mail docks, at the foot of Brannan Street in San Francisco. On July 25, 1877, this was the scene of a violent battle between Workingmen's Party supporters and city police. Because it transported Chinese laborers from the Orient to San Francisco, the Pacific Mail Steamship Company was often the target of anti-Chinese groups. C. E. Watkins photograph. (*California Historical Society*.) **This page, top:** Cartoon (1876) from *The Wasp*, a satirical, highly racist newspaper published in San Francisco during the 1870's and 1880's. The Rev. Otis Gibson and the Rev. August Loomis were San Francisco clergymen who were vocal defenders of the Chinese. (*California Historical Society*.) **This page, bottom:** Portion of the Workingmen's Party ticket in the Alameda County elections, 1878. Using Kearney's slogan, "The Chinese must go!," the Workingmen's Party elected candidates in both Alameda and Sacramento Counties that year. (*California State Library*.)

The Development of Chinatown

Above: Cartoon entitled "In the clutches of the Chinese tiger" from *The Wasp*, November 7, 1885. Exclusionists warned that ignoring the "yellow peril" could have dire consequences. (*California Historical Society.*) **Opposite, top:** Chinatown at the time of the Exclusion Act was six blocks long, from California to Broadway, and two blocks wide, from Kearny to Stockton. This view was taken at the corner of Sacramento and Dupont Street (now Grant Avenue) looking west. (*Bancroft Library.*)

Opposite, bottom: Officers of the Chinese Six Companies, ca. 1890. The Chinese Six Companies, whose official title is the Chinese Consolidated Benevolent Association, was formed from the major district associations. Its function included arbitrating disputes between districts, caring for the aged, and burying the dead. It also had the power to speak on behalf of the Chinese community in California and to initiate programs concerning their welfare. (*Bancroft Library.*)

Left: Associations called tongs, made up of immigrants who had no strong family or district ties, were originally formed for the same benevolent purposes as other Chinese associations. However, they gradually moved into the more lucrative areas of gambling, narcotics, prostitution, extortion and slavery. This tong official is followed closely by his bodyguard, who, hand in pocket, keeps a watchful eye around him. Genthe photograph. (*California Historical Society.*) **Right:** These three men were convicted burglars. The photographs are taken from a Chinese rogues' gallery compiled by San Francisco police officer Delos Woodruff from 1868 to 1871. Captions read: "Wong Ah Wing, 10 years," "Ah Foock, 7 years" and "Ah Ping, ali[as] Cat." (*California Historical Society.*) **Opposite:** Arnold Genthe and Tea Rose, a young protégée of Donaldina Cameron. Genthe, a native of Berlin, came to San Francisco in 1895 as the tutor to the son of a German baron. He took up photography when his efforts to sketch scenes in Chinatown were unsatisfactory. Though he is best known for his warm, charming photographs of Chinatown, he was also a fine portraitist. Genthe lost almost all his possessions in the fire of 1906, but his Chinatown negatives survived, thanks to Will Irwin's warning two years previously: "You really ought not to keep these plates and films here. Someday the whole city will burn up. There'll never be another Chinatown like this one, and you have its only picture record." Genthe placed the negatives in a friend's vault and thus preserved a lost era for posterity. (*California Historical Society.*)

Looking down on a parade scene in Chinatown, probably on Dupont Street. Note the people standing on rooftops, balconies, and—seemingly unconcerned—on ledges and canopies. Taber photograph. (*Society of California Pioneers.*)

Left: A passerby checks out a shop window. He is wearing the typical workingman's garb—loose tunic and trousers of blue cotton—and a Western hat. Genthe photograph. (*California Historical Society.*) **Right:** Chinese dentist's office, the toothy symbols advertising his trade. The sign below reads: "Repair Shop: Umbrellas, Porcelain Chinaware.") (*Society of California Pioneers.*) **Opposite, top:** A lily vendor holds up two plants for inspection. Many Chinese flower growers had small farms south of San Francisco and came into town periodically to sell their wares. In later years, when the area became urbanized, flower growers retreated south to San Mateo and Santa Clara Counties. Genthe photograph. (*California Historical Society.*) **Opposite, bottom:** A Chinese pharmacist carefully weighs the ingredients for a prescription. The unmarked drawers behind him hold the herbs and preparations necessary for his trade. The Chinese used drugs such as quinine, digitalis and ephedrine long before Westerners discovered their value. (*Wells Fargo Bank History Room.*)

Top: A shoemaker in his open-air shop. Chinese workers were also employed on a large scale in boot and shoe factories in San Francisco; in 1873 50% of the shoes produced in California were made by Chinese. (*Wells Fargo History Room.*) **Bottom:** "The Balloon Man," by Arnold Genthe. The little boy is dressed in holiday attire; his queue is made mostly of braided silk cord. (*California Historical Society.*)

Top: "The Tinkers," by Arnold Genthe. Chinatown was full of itinerant tradesmen who needed only a small corner for their activities. (*California Historical Society.*) **Bottom:** Fish market, Chinatown. The Chinese established numerous fishing camps in the San Francisco area. Genthe photograph. (*California Historical Society.*)

Top: A long-haired quartet in Chinatown around the turn of the century. The queue was imposed upon the Chinese as a sign of subjugation when the Manchus took power in China in 1644. Rev. Otis Gibson commented wryly, "There was no compulsion, however. Persons who did not like the innovation were at liberty to refuse ... the penalty being simply the loss of their heads." Later, the queue became a fixed and accepted fashion among Chinese men. (*California Historical Society.*) **Bottom:** These two children are ready for a holiday; one has already visited the balloon man, the other covers her ears to shut out the noise of the firecrackers. In the background, their elders read the latest notices. Genthe photograph. (*California Historical Society.*) **Opposite, top, left:** A Chinese laborer poses, queue in hand. This was an unusual hairstyle; the acceptable fashion was to shave the front of the head. The political heroes pinned to the man's breast—Grover Cleveland and his running mate Allen G. Thurman—indicate that the photo was taken in the election year of 1888. (*California State Library.*) **Opposite, top, right:** Chinese fortune teller. The sticks in the cylindrical box were painted with Chinese characters. Clients shook the box with a circular motion until one of the sticks slipped out, and the fortune teller then interpreted the markings on that particular stick. (*Wells Fargo Bank History Room.*) **Opposite, bottom:** A pair of children at the corner of Dupont and Jackson Streets, ca. 1900. Note the now-defunct cable car line on Jackson. Genthe photograph. (*California Historical Society.*)

Opposite, top: Employees of a butcher and grocery shop in Chinatown pause for a moment to be photographed. Men of the working class often coiled their queues around their heads while on the job, but it was said that aristocrats would never think of doing so. Taber photograph. (*Bancroft Library*.) **Opposite, bottom:** Public letter writer, San Francisco. Very few of the early immigrants were literate; they employed public scribes to correspond with their families in the old country. (*California Historical Society*.) **Above:** Not all facets of Chinatown were picturesque. Overcrowding, substandard housing and disease—still problems faced by modern-day Chinatown—were common. Tenement house; Taber photograph, ca. 1888. (*California Historical Society*.)

Top, left: Taken at a time when Chinese had few contacts with whites—and then usually in a servant–employer context—this is a most unusual photograph. In studio portraits of that era, the dominant figure (the husband or father) was the one who was seated. (*California Historical Society*.) **Top, right:** "Children of High Class," by Arnold Genthe. The man in the photograph was Lew Kan, an imposing man who stood well over six feet tall, thus accounting for his frequent appearance in photos of the period. He is accompanied here by his sons, Lew Bing You (center) and Lew Bing Yuen (right), who are dressed for a holiday. Lew Kan was a merchant who operated a store called Fook On Lung, on Sacramento Street between Dupont (now Grant) and Kearny, and he later owned a store in Fresno, the Sing Chong Lung Kan Kee Company, at 1520 Tulare Street. Although all three Lews are now deceased, their descendants still live in the San Francisco and Fresno areas. (*California Historical Society*.) **Bottom:** Interior of a Chinese barber shop. "The Celestial sits on a common chair ... then the queue is unbraided the silk taken out of it ... then his hair is twisted into a knot, the head and face is then washed in warm water ... first the head is shaved, then the face, forehead and ears ... with a long thin knife" (George B. Morris). No lather was used, and considerable attention was paid to the rebraiding of the queue. Silk cord was used to fill it out, with an obligatory tassel left on the end. (*San Francisco Public Library*.)

After Hours:
Mah-Jongg and Missionaries

A group of Chinese actors in full dress. There were no women in the acting profession; the sweet young thing at the far left was a man, specially trained since childhood to imitate women's mannerisms. (*J. S. Holliday Collection.*)

Top: Interior of a Chinese theater on Jackson Street. Most theaters had a seating capacity of several hundred and reserved one of the galleries for women. Rev. Otis Gibson observed: "The stage has no flies, shifting scenes, or drop curtain, but is simply an elevated platform, with two doors at the rear, through which the actors make their entrance and exit." He also described the manner of exit: "A slain person lies in this way [with a block of wood under his head] until the end of the scene, when he coolly arises and walks off the stage in full view of the entire audience." (*California Historical Society.*) **Bottom:** "Chinese theatricals do not show much dancing, yet they do sometimes exhibit rare feats in tumbling, jumping, turning cart-wheels, etc." (Gibson, *The Chinese in America*). This photograph was taken ca. 1890 at the St. Louis Art Studio in San Francisco, whose advertisement reads "Children's portraits a specialty." It is unclear whether the boy is a genuine acrobat or is merely using a studio prop. (*California Historical Society.*) **Opposite:** "Street of the Gamblers," by Arnold Genthe. Gambling—fan tan, pai gow, Mah-Jongg and lotteries—was a popular pastime in Chinatown. This rare, uncropped version of the picture is signed by the photographer. (*California Historical Society.*)

Opposite, top: Chinese gamblers playing Mah-Jongg, an ancient game using marked tiles which are drawn and discarded until one player has a winning hand. Prostitutes often frequented the Mah-Jongg rooms in hopes of finding clients. (*Thomas W. Chinn Collection.*) **Opposite, bottom:** Opium den, San Francisco, ca. 1900. Opium smuggling flourished until the 1920's, when the Chinatown Squad of the San Francisco Police Depart-ment began a tough campaign of law enforcement. (*California Historical Society.*) **Above:** The San Francisco Police Department's Raiding Squad in the 1890's, pictured with an inter-preter and the tools of their trade: axes, ropes and sledge-hammers. The Raiding Squad was formed in 1875 and was the forerunner of the Chinatown Squad. (*Bancroft Library.*)

Above: Interior of a Chinese joss house, San Francisco, showing five deities. The word "joss" is a corruption of the Portuguese *Deus*, meaning "God." Chinese temples are nondenominational, welcoming all worshipers. The first temple to be built in San Francisco was probably the Kong Chow Temple, which was destroyed by fire in 1906 and rebuilt five years afterward. Taber photograph. (*California Historical Society*.) **Opposite, top:** This photograph shows a mixture of Chinese and Western culture. The wedding party is dressed traditionally in Chinese attire, but the ceremony took place at the Presbyterian Mission. The bride was a pupil of Donaldina Cameron's. Left to right: best man, groom, servant, bride, brother, two sisters, parents and child servant. Stellman photograph. (*Bancroft Library*.) **Opposite, bottom:** Members of the Chinese Salvation Army pray together on the cobblestoned streets of Chinatown. Genthe photograph. (*California Historical Society*.)

Opposite, top, left: The Foke Yam Tong ("Gospel Temple"), better known as the Chinese Methodist Chapel. Services were held daily at two in the afternoon, all in Chinese; the attendance at the Sunday sessions was estimated at forty. Bible and hymnbook were the only books used. From a stereoscopic view. (*Society of California Pioneers.*) **Opposite, top, right:** These fashionable young women were photographed in San Francisco ca. 1915, possibly on their way to Sunday school. The photo was taken by Mervyn D. Silberstein, a photographer of the post-earthquake period who specialized in views of Chinatown. His photographs were heavily retouched to increase their commercial value—signs in English were obliterated and replaced with "calligraphy," designs were added to clothing to make them appear more Chinese. However, his original, unaltered photographs are warm and charming. (*Gloria Brown Collection; Gloria Brown is the daughter of the photographer.*) **Opposite, bottom:** Chinese funeral, San Francisco, ca. 1900. Traditional funerals inevitably attracted crowds of curious onlookers. Frank Norris, writing for *The Wave* in 1897, described an extreme case at the funeral of Little Pete, Chinatown's millionaire gangster: "The civilized Americans, some thousand of them, descended upon the raised platform, where the funeral meats were placed. . . . Four men seized a roast pig by either leg and made off with it. . . . The roast chickens were hurled back and forth. The women scrambled for the china bowls as souvenirs of the occasion." (*California Historical Society.*) **This page, top:** For many years the Chinese were barred from burying their dead in existing cemeteries, so they established their own. The major Chinese cemetery was in Colma, south of San Francisco, but there was once a Chinese seamen's cemetery in Lincoln Park, near the present Legion of Honor. It was customary to exhume the body after a number of years and send the bones back to China for burial; this method was neater and less expensive than shipping the entire body. In this photograph, people are touching up the writing on wooden tombstones at Colma. On Ch'ing Ming (Pure Brightness Festival), the Chinese equivalent of Memorial Day, it is traditional for all Chinese to visit the cemeteries and *sao mu*—literally, sweep the graves. The graves are tended and swept with willow branches to drive off harmful spirits, and food and floral offerings are left before them. Stellman photograph. (*California State Library.*) **This page, bottom:** At Chinese funerals, paper gifts (houses, money, servants, horses) were burned to provide for the deceased in the afterlife, and sweet incense was used to propitiate the gods. Drums, horns, cymbals and firecrackers were used to ward off harmful spirits, and paper money was strewn along the path to the cemetery to pacify them. There were stores in Chinatown which specialized in funeral supplies. (*Wells Fargo Bank History Room.*)

New Era:
Death of Old Chinatown

Opposite: A lone man surveys the wreckage of Chinatown after the earthquake and fire of 1906. It was rebuilt in the same location, but some said it was never again the same "gaily painted, and proverbially wicked" place that it had been. The building in the distance, its dome falling over, was the Hall of Justice on Kearny Street near Portsmouth Square. Genthe photograph. (*California Historical Society.*) **This page, top:** California Street, from Montgomery to Kearny, where the Bank of America World Headquarters building now stands. Two residents of Chinatown make their way up the hill, possibly en route to a refugee camp, while behind them, crowds of people rush to the ferry. Many of the Chinese who found refuge in Oakland and other cities never returned; Chinatown's population after the earthquake decreased from 15,000 to 10,000. (*California Historical Society.*) **This page, bottom:** "When earthquake tumbled down your heavy cornices and unstable chimneys and set in motion flames that burned your home to the ground, who of your household was it who came with a gold-filled purse to tide over emergencies? Likely as not, it was faithful Sing" (Charles Caldwell Dobie, *San Francisco's Chinatown*). This photograph shows a Chinese cook, Lum, in his makeshift kitchen at 2108 Sutter Street, shortly after the earthquake. (*Oakland Museum.*)

Opposite, top, left: Mr. and Mrs. Fong Wan and their sons, Richard and Ed, ca. 1910. Fong later became Oakland's leading herbalist. (*Oakland Museum.*) **Opposite, top, right:** A small parade watcher in readiness. Stellman photograph. (*California State Library.*) **Opposite, bottom, left:** Two Chinese immigrants aboard ship, probably a merchant and his wife. The Exclusion Act of 1882 prohibited the immigration of Chinese laborers for a period of ten years; in 1892 it was extended for ten years, and in 1902, for another ten years. (*Bancroft Library.*) **Opposite, bottom, right:** Two boys salute the country of their birth. Stellman photograph. Louis J. Stellman treated the Chinese with compassion rather than as oddities or objects of contempt. Like Genthe and other pictorialists, he used a soft focus and preferred candid shots to stiff studio poses. His work was never retouched. (*California State Library.*) **Above:** A native son solemnly regards his cigar-chomping father. Only the father-and-son portion of this picture was sold commercially. Silberstein photograph. (*Gloria Brown Collection.*)

Top, left: This photograph demonstrates the Westernization of clothing that was taking place. Although her father wears his hair in a queue, the little girl resembles any other young lady of the time. Genthe photograph. (*California Historical Society.*) **Top, right:** This grave young man in knickers and button shoes pauses in his travels for a minute. Although automobiles were beginning to make their appearance, horse-drawn wagons like the one in the background were more common. Silberstein photograph. (*Gloria Brown Collection.*) **Bottom:** There were also Chinese photographers operating in San Francisco during the post-earthquake period, as evidenced by the logo on this portrait. The man in the photograph was Tin Low, a servant in the household of Mrs. James de Barth Shorb. (*California Historical Society.*) **Opposite:** Two sisters enjoy a quiet moment by a flower stand. The woman on the right is Mrs. Chang Wah Lee; the woman on the left was herself a photographer and, with her husband, ran the Sao Yung Studio (formerly May's Studio) on Sacramento Street. Silberstein photograph. (*Gloria Brown Collection.*)

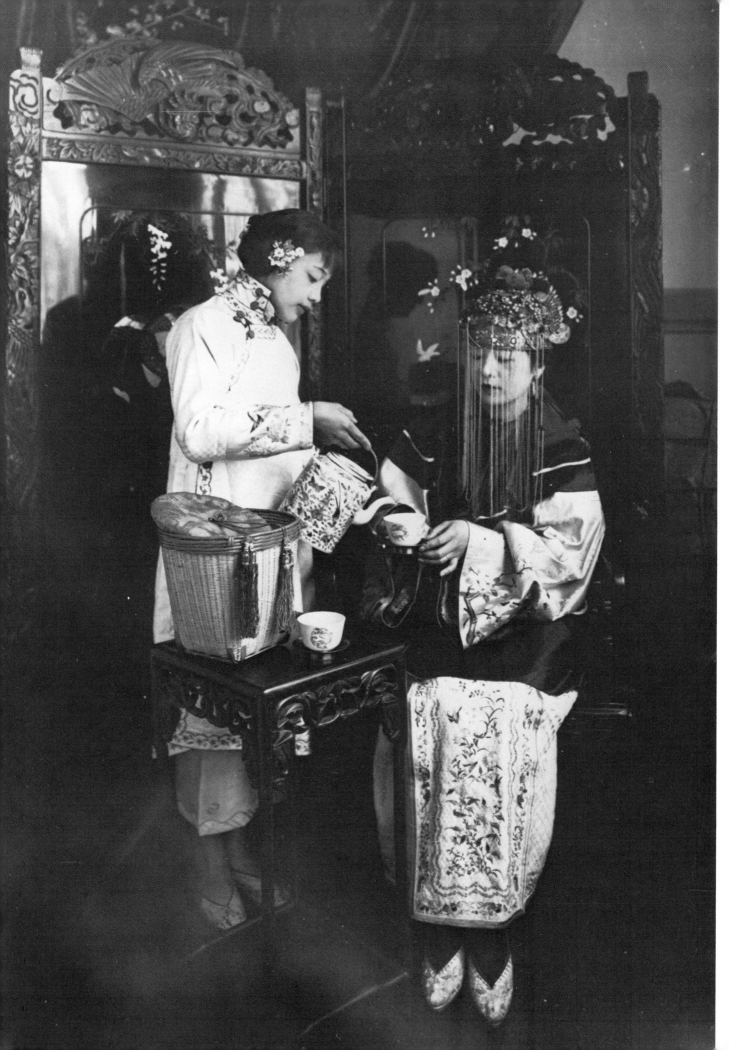

Opposite: Tea ceremony preceding a traditional Chinese marriage. Here the maid, dressed in her finest, pours tea for the bride, who will in turn serve her fiancé's parents. (*Gloria Brown Collection.*) **Above:** The Sam Hop Company, 815 Clay Street, San Francisco, 1908. Note the woman behind the counter of this general import store. Chinese women in the United States eventually occupied a higher standing than that of women in China, because of the scarcity of women here and the prevalence of small businesses in which wives were working partners. (*California Historical Society.*)

Top: From a postcard dated December 31, 1910. The message, addressed to a Miss Mary Edwards, 727 Stockton Street, San Francisco, reads: "A Happy new year. wishes to you. I hope you the cold all will well. I and my frend the picture. from Woo Dum." (*California Historical Society.*) **Bottom:** An old man dozes near baskets of eggs and crabs. Before crab fishing on the Pacific Coast became organized, the Chinese caught crabs off the San Francisco wharves with strong circular nets and sold them for 75 cents per dozen. (*California Historical Society.*)

Top: By 1910 there were four Chinese dailies published in San Francisco. The editor of the *Chung Sai Yat Po*, Ng Poon Chew, was one of the best-known English-speaking Chinese on the West Coast. Stellman photograph. (*California State Library.*)
Bottom: Four men stand in front of the Pow Hing Company, Groceries & General Merchandise. The signs behind them reflect the change in the goods sold by Chinese stores. (*Society of California Pioneers.*)

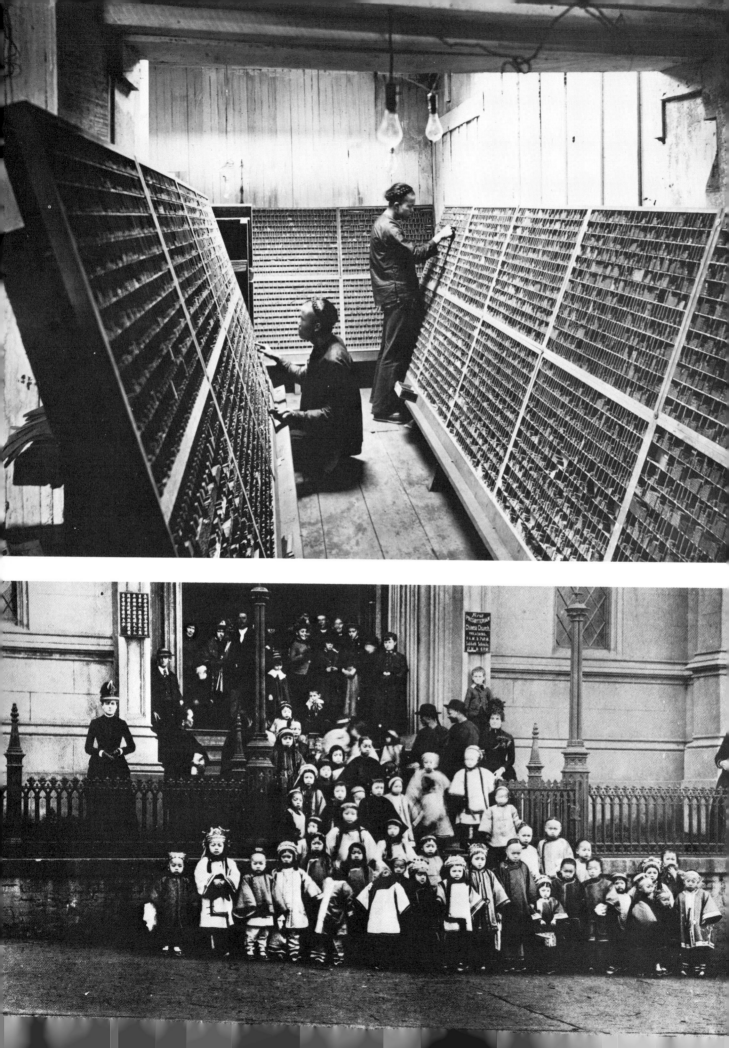

Opposite, top: Setting the type for a Chinese newspaper was an ambitious undertaking. Approximately 12,000 characters were kept on hand, and special characters were added from time to time, custom-made by a Chinese engraver. During the 1906 fire, all existing Chinese news plants were destroyed, and there was then a lapse of eight months while the newspapers waited for new type to arrive from China. (*Robert Weinstein Collection.*) Opposite, bottom: Miss Cable's class of Chinese girls, First Presbyterian Church, ca. 1882. Aside from church-run schools such as these, there were few efforts made to provide education for the Chinese. A separate facility for Chinese children was established in San Francisco in 1887, but no attempts were made to modernize it. The Chinese, realizing that their options were limited, formed their own schools, teaching Chinese language, history and classics. For years it was customary to send American-born children to China to further their education. Taber photograph. (*California Historical Society.*) Above: The Republic of China was founded in October of 1911, and Sun Yat-sen, who operated out of San Francisco, was chosen as its first president. The Chinese revolution was financed mainly through contributions from overseas Chinese. Stellman photograph. (*California State Library.*)

Top: Tom Gunn expresses his pleasure upon winning an air race at the Curtiss School of Aviation in San Diego. Gunn, a well-known aviator, died in a plane crash in China in 1912. A Bay Area Chinese, Fung Joe Guey, made the first heavier-than-air flight on the West Coast in 1909. (*California Historical Society.*) **Bottom:** The characters at the left identify this early Chinese aviator as Lum Fook Yuen. Stellman photograph. (*California State Library.*) **Opposite:** An unidentified parade through Chinatown. One of San Francisco's finest, at the left, paces the lead horse. (*California Historical Society.*)

Second Generation

Opposite: Burning confiscated opium in Chinatown, ca. 1919. Before 1921, when John J. Manion was appointed to head the Chinatown Squad, narcotics trafficking, gambling and commercialized sex were rampant. (*Society of California Pioneers.*) **This page, top:** Jack Manion displays buckets and tins with false bottoms, shoes with hollow heels, and opium pipes which the Chinatown Squad confiscated. Using rough tactics, Manion succeeded in eradicating opium smuggling in Chinatown. (*San Francisco Public Library.*) **This page, bottom:** "We used to keep axes, and crowbars, and sledgehammers stored in a wooden box we had wired to a telephone pole on Waverly Place between Sacramento and Clay streets. We'd go and get a couple of axes and crowbars and bust in" (former member of the Chinatown Squad, as quoted in Jerry Flamm's *Good Life in Hard Times*). Pictured are Sgt. Harry Walsh, Manion's predecessor (left, standing), George Hipley (right) and Tommy Hyland (kneeling). (*San Francisco Public Library.*)

Above: A group of parents with their children at a well-baby clinic in San Francisco, 1928. Because immigration was difficult before the "paper son" influx, Chinatown's second generation did not make its appearance until the 1920's. (*California Historical Society.*) **Opposite, top:** Looking very much like a row of kewpie dolls, the first Miss Chinatown, Ella Dong, and her court reign over the 1925 pageant. (*Chinese Historical Society of America.*) **Opposite, bottom:** The Chinese YMCA conducted the same activities as the American YMCA. In addition, they offered free English lessons and operated kindergartens. In 1923 there were five Chinese YMCAs and three Chinese YWCAs in the United States (*Thomas W. Chinn Collection.*)

Top: Class of 1926, Yeung Wo Chinese School, San Francisco. Until the Sino-Japanese War in the 1930's, it was customary for parents to send their children back to China to complete their education. Chinese-language schools in this country acted as "prep" schools. (*Thomas W. Chinn Collection.*) **Bottom:** Yeung Wo Chinese School basketball team, San Francisco, 1924. Young people born in the United States had become Americanized, adopting the fashions and interests typical of their generation, but they were still viewed as Chinese by the outside community. (*Thomas W. Chinn Collection.*) **Opposite, top:** New Year's celebration in Oakland's Chinatown, February 12, 1927, heralding the year 3700. Since 1851, when the first Chinese New Year's observance was held in San Francisco, this had become a major festival in Chinese communities in California. (*California Historical Society.*) **Opposite, bottom:** Angel Island, now a 720-acre state park, was the immigration detention center for San Francisco from 1909 to 1949. Ostensibly a quarantine station for immigrants from Asia and the Pacific, it actually was a means of detaining Chinese immigrants for indefinite periods. The walls at Angel Island still display bitter poetry written by detainees. During 1920 alone, over 20,000 travelers were processed at the center. (*California Historical Society.*)

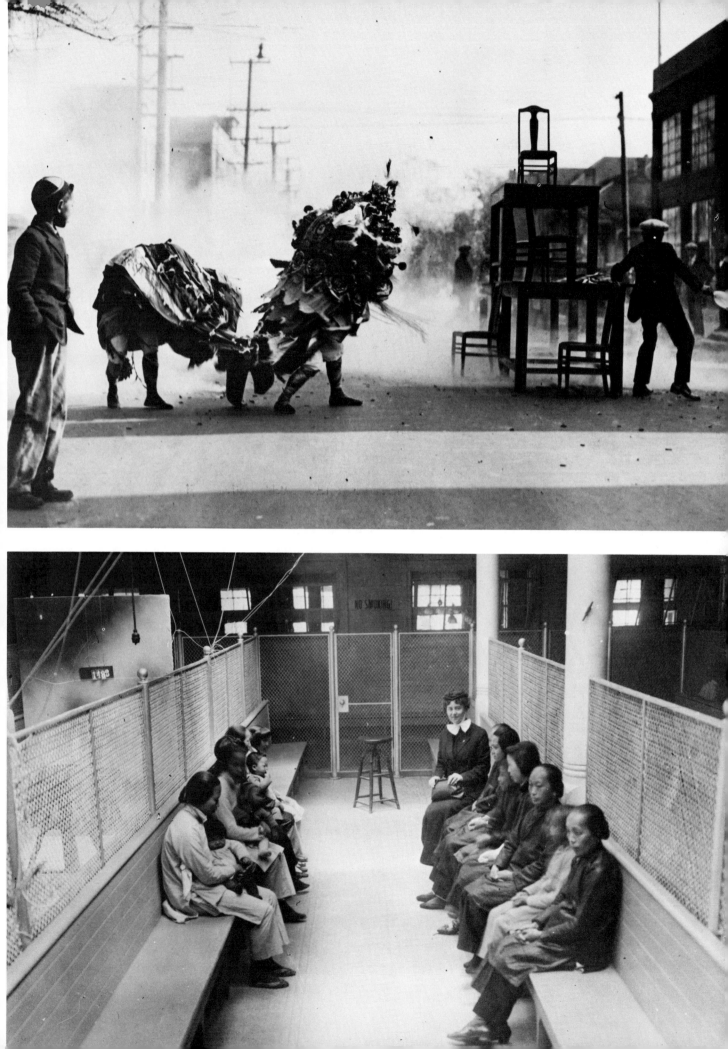

The War Years

Above: The playground of the Chinese nursery school and kindergarten in San Francisco, 1934. This school was one of the first of its kind, established with public funds. (*San Francisco Public Library*.) **Opposite, top:** Leo Chan, his wife and son pose proudly with their luxurious automobile. Chan was a portrait photographer in San Francisco for over 30 years. (*George C. Berticevich Collection*.) **Opposite, bottom:** Boys in San Francisco, 1935, celebrate Chinese New Year's with firecrackers. (*San Francisco Public Library*.)

Top: A view of Chinatown in the 1930's, looking down Grant Avenue, which has been the main artery of Chinatown since the early days. (*California Historical Society.*) **Bottom:** Inside a Chinese laundry, 1937. The man in the back is using brush-painted characters to identify the customer's laundry: "man who squints," "lady with many husbands," etc. (*San Francisco Public Library.*) **Opposite, top:** This charming view of boys building a sand pyramid in Chinatown was released as a publicity photograph by the San Francisco Chamber of Commerce in the early 1930's. (*California Historical Society.*) **Opposite, bottom:** Chinese workmen bagging onions on the San Francisco docks, 1934. The Pacific Coast maritime strike began that year, later developing into the San Francisco general strike. (*San Francisco Maritime Museum.*)

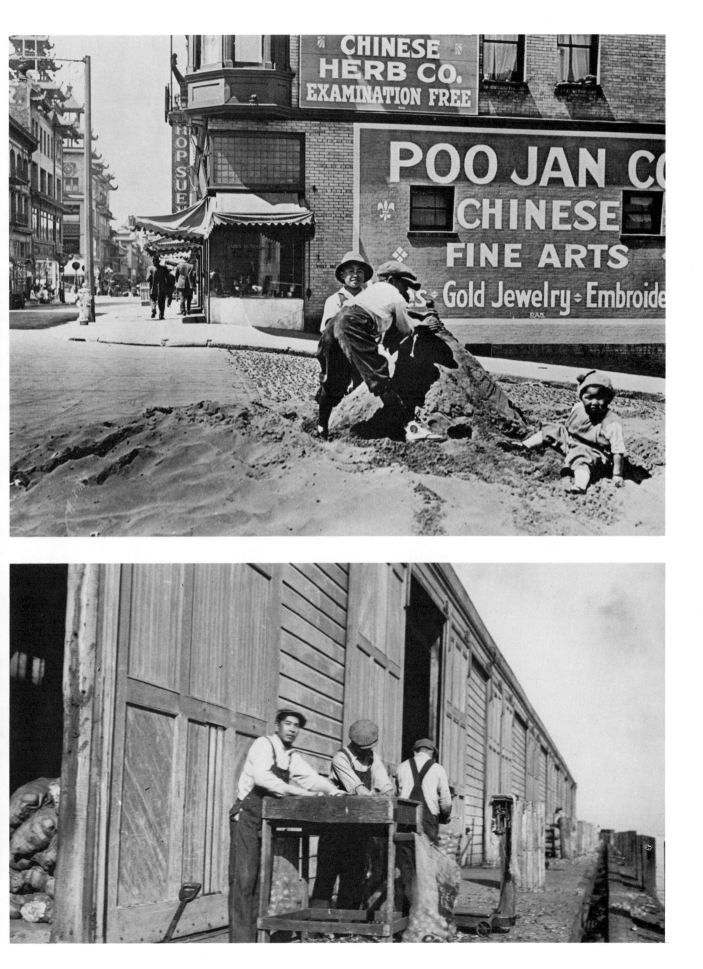

108 THE CHINESE IN SAN FRANCISCO

Opposite: The Chinese Telephone Exchange on Washington Street between Brenham Place and Grant Avenue, undoubtedly the most distinctive of the Pacific Telephone Company's branches. (*San Francisco Public Library*.) **This page, top:** A view of the interior of the Chinese Telephone Exchange. Only Chinese-speaking women were hired as operators, and all calls in Chinatown were routed through this switchboard. (*Bancroft Library*.) **This page, bottom:** The Chinese Telephone Exchange produced and distributed a special directory, handwritten in Chinese. Here a calligrapher painstakingly completes a page in the directory. (*Chinese Historical Society of America*.)

Top: A trio of youngsters wait patiently for the trained lark to select their fortunes from the box on which it is perched. The fortune-telling lark was one of the most popular attractions at the Chinese Village, Golden Gate International Exposition, 1939. (*California Historical Society*.) **Bottom:** San Francisco Mayor Angelo Rossi and George Jue (with scroll) at a ceremony promoting the Chinese pavilion at the Golden Gate International Exposition, 1939. Jue was later president of the Chinese Chamber of Commerce. (*California Historical Society*.) **Opposite:** Golden Gate International Exposition, Treasure Island, 1939. To most American-born Chinese visitors, the Chinese Village was as new and exciting as any other foreign pavilion at the fair. (*California Historical Society*.)

Opposite, top: Following World War I, Japan began to pursue expansionist policies in Asia, and in the 1930's war broke out between China and Japan. In San Francisco, concerned Chinese flocked to newspaper offices to read the latest bulletins. (*California Historical Society.*) **Opposite, bottom:** The Japanese attack on Pearl Harbor brought the United States into the war and, for the first time, the Chinese and white communities were united against a common enemy. These men are shown registering at the Chinese consulate general, 551 Montgomery Street, San Francisco, to avoid being mistaken for Japanese. (*San Francisco Public Library.*) **Above:** San Francisco Chinese were active in the war effort. The Rice Bowl Party pictured, May 1941, was one of many benefits organized to raise money for Chinese war refugees. (*San Francisco Public Library.*)

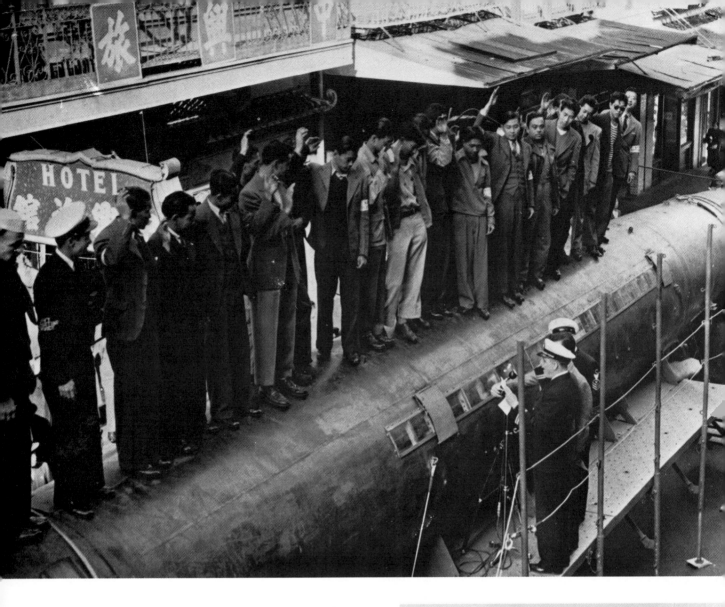

Top: This Japanese submarine, captured after Pearl Harbor, was on a nation-wide tour. Here Chinese naval recruits line up and take their oath as part of Navy Day ceremonies in San Francisco, January 1942. World War II marked the first opportunity for Chinese men to compete on an equal basis with their white contemporaries. (*San Francisco Public Library*.) **Bottom:** Mrs. Tse Kei-Yuen (left) and Mrs. Len Sen, volunteer workers in Chinatown's War Chest campaign, 1943. The Chinese community had set $13,000 as their goal. (*San Francisco Public Library*.)

Top: San Francisco schoolgirls buying war bonds, 1943. Left to right: Anna Chew, Shirley Young, Claudia Lew, Roberta Chew, Carol Ann Loo, Sylvia Dunn, Frances Poon. Overseas Chinese bought over $500 million in war bonds during the Sino-Japanese War and continued to contribute throughout World War II. (*San Francisco Public Library.*) **Bottom:** During the 1940's San Francisco Chinese made more than just monetary contributions to the war effort. Here, in a four-part self-portrait, Leo Chan models his air-raid warden's uniform and gas mask. (*George C. Berticevich Collection.*)

THE WAR YEARS   115

Opposite: The California Street cable car passes through the intersection of California and Grant Avenue, 1945. Chinatown by then had become very progressive, with modern buildings and store fronts, but it still retained a Chinese flavor. Photograph by Paul Henchey. (*Bancroft Library*.) **This page, top:** Corporal Tommy Yee, wounded while serving with the Philippine Liberation Forces, shares his experiences with a rapt audience, 1945. Left to right: Michael Wong, Suzette Chin and Rosalind Chin. (*San Francisco Public Library*.) **This page, bottom:** USO dance at the Chinese YWCA, 1945. Although the war brought about increased fraternization between Chinese and Caucasians, California's anti-miscegenation law was not abolished until 1948. (*San Francisco Public Library*.)

Above: Representatives of the Chinese Young Women's Society of Oakland, Rosebud Mye (left) and Dr. Eugenia Mye (right), accept the War Service Award from Commander Andrew C. Wong of the American Legion's Cathay Post. (*California Historical Society*.) **Opposite, top:** A group of Chinese youngsters listen attentively to Sister Mary Pius in a Chinese school, 1948. (*California Historical Society*.) **Opposite, bottom:** A Chinatown apartment—cited as a typical example of substandard housing in the District Attorney's report, 1947—where eight people occupied two rooms. In 1948 the law prohibiting Chinese from owning homes outside of Chinatown was repealed, and many families relocated in San Francisco's Richmond and Sunset districts. (*San Francisco Public Library*.)

Postwar to the Present

Opposite: Private Henry Yum of San Francisco, a student in the Fort Ord Leaders course, checks his appearance before leaving the barracks, July 1951. (*California Historical Society.*) **This page, top:** Christmas parade, San Francisco Chinatown, 1951. Dorothy Lee waves from a flower-bedecked float. (*California Historical Society.*) **This page, bottom:** This young cowboy, a member of the "American Chinese" generation, was probably more familiar with the adventures of Roy Rogers and Hopalong Cassidy than with the teachings of Chinese philosophers. Chan photograph. (*George C. Berticevich Collection.*)

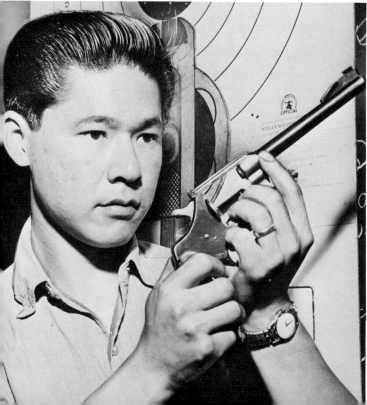

Top: Dedication of the Ping Yuen housing project on Pacific Avenue between Grant and Columbus, 1951. 600 applications were received for 234 apartments of 1, 2 or 3 bedrooms. They originally rented for $15 to $60 per month, depending upon income. Housing has always been a problem in overcrowded Chinatown. (*San Francisco Public Library.*) **Bottom:** Herbert Lee, the first Chinese on the San Francisco police force, checks his weapon, 1957. (*California Historical Society.*) **Opposite, top:** St. Mary's Drum and Bugle Corps, a prizewinning group from the Chinese Catholic mission in San Francisco, performs for an appreciative audience, 1960. (*California Historical Society.*) **Opposite, bottom:** Presidential candidate John F. Kennedy is greeted by enthusiastic supporters, including a contingent from Chinatown, at San Francisco International Airport, September 1960. Later, as President, Kennedy signed a law that permitted increased immigration from Hong Kong. (*Chinese Historical Society of America.*)

Top: The Yim family partakes in the first meal of the New Year, February 1962. The third generation, mostly raised in the suburbs and speaking English as a first language, became comfortable in two cultures. (*San Francisco Public Library.*) **Bottom:** A worker in a fortune-cookie factory, Chinatown, 1970's. These factories, like the notorious garment factories, operate late into the night. (*San Francisco Chronicle Publishing Company.*)

Top: The Gateway to Chinatown, at Grant and Bush, photographed in 1969. Chinatown, by the end of the 1960's, occupied 42 blocks. Photograph by Vincent Maggiora. (*San Francisco Chronicle Publishing Company.*) **Bottom:** The dismantling of Kong Chow Temple, 1969. The temple, possibly the first built in San Francisco, was moved from 520 Pine Street to Stockton Street, where it was rededicated in 1978. (*Thomas W. Chinn Collection.*)

Above: Shoppers on Grant Avenue, 1972. Although in many ways a typical city street, Grant Avenue still has open markets offering Chinese vegetables, hanging sides of pork and dressed ducks, sausages and fresh fish. The sidewalks are always crowded with pedestrians and tourists. Photograph by Arthur Frisch. (*San Francisco Chronicle Publishing Company.*) **Opposite, top:** Chinese garment workers on strike, 1968, at 5 Stark Alley, on Stockton between Pacific and Broadway. Attempts to organize workers from the garment factories have been unsuccessful to date. (*Chinese Historical Society of America.*) **Opposite, bottom:** Chinatown rent pickets, 660 Sacramento Street, May 1977. In the 1970's even the elderly residents of Chinatown, traditionally unprotesting, participated in demonstrations for better housing and health care. The best-publicized of these demonstrations involved the International Hotel, whose residents—mainly elderly Chinese and Filipino men—were evicted when the owners of the building decided to tear it down. Photograph by Joseph J. Rosenthal. (*San Francisco Chronicle Publishing Company.*)

Opposite, top: The old men who gather on the benches at Portsmouth Square are remnants of the period before immigration laws were lifted, when Chinatown was mainly a bachelor society. Photograph, 1976, by Gary Fong. (*San Francisco Chronicle Publishing Company.*) **Opposite, bottom, left:** Plaque presented by the Chinese Historical Society of America to commemorate the centennial of the transcontinental railroad, 1969. Pictured left to right are Philip P. Choy, Chinese Consul General Chou, San Francisco Supervisor Peter Tamaras, and Thomas W. Chinn, who assists his mother, 98-year-old Mrs. Chinn Lee Shee Wing. (*Thomas W. Chinn Collection.*) **Opposite, bottom, right:** Members of the first immigrant gang in Chinatown, the Wah Ching (China Youth), playing cards, ca. 1970. Formed in 1968, the Wah Ching was originally begun as a social club and job corps. (*California Historical Society.*) **This page, top:** A Chinese street musician and his captivated listener, San Francisco, 1976. Photograph by Vincent Maggiora. (*San Francisco Chronicle Publishing Company.*) **This page, bottom:** Willie Woo, the "Rhinestone King," 1971. The Third World and ethnic-pride movements of the late 1960's have made Chinatown's third generation, the American Chinese, aware of their unique heritage and history. (*California Historical Society.*)

Overleaf: For the Chinese in San Francisco, as with any group, the future is in the hands of the young, but they have come to realize that the key to their future is inextricably linked with their past. Cityscape, 1960's, with the Coit Tower atop Telegraph Hill (left), Yerba Buena Island and the Bay Bridge, as seen from Russian Hill. (*California Historical Society.*)

Bibliography

BOOKS

Bancroft, Hubert Howe, *History of California*, volumes VI (1848–1859) and VII (1860–1890), History Company Publishers, San Francisco, 1888.

Barth, Gunther, *Bitter Strength: A History of the Chinese in the U.S., 1850–1870*, Harvard University Press, Cambridge, 1964.

Chapman, Charles, *A History of California*, Macmillan, New York, 1921.

Chinn, Thomas W.; Lai, H. Mark; and Choy, Philip P., *A History of the Chinese in California*, Chinese Historical Society of America, San Francisco, 1969.

Chu, Daniel; and Chu, Samuel, *Passage to the Golden Gate*, Doubleday & Company, New York, 1967.

Coolidge, Mary Roberts, *Chinese Immigration*, Henry Holt & Company, New York, 1909.

Dobie, Charles Caldwell, *San Francisco's Chinatown*, D. Appleton-Century Company, New York, 1936.

Eldredge, Zoeth Skinner, *History of California*, volume 4, Century History Company, New York, 1915.

Flamm, Jerry, *Good Life in Hard Times: San Francisco in the '20s and '30s*, Chronicle Books, San Francisco, 1978.

Genthe, Arnold, *As I Remember*, Reynal & Hitchcock, New York, 1936.

Gibson, (Rev.) Otis, *The Chinese in America*, Hitchcock & Walden, Cincinnati, 1877.

Hom, Gloria Sun, *Chinese Argonauts: An Anthology of the Chinese Contributions to the Historical Development of Santa Clara County*, Foothill Community College, Los Altos, 1971.

Hoy, William, *The Chinese Six Companies*, Chinese Consolidated Benevolent Association, San Francisco, 1942.

Hsu, Francis L. K., *The Challenge of the American Dream: The Chinese in the United States*, Wadsworth Publishing Company, Belmont, 1971.

Irwin, Will, *Old Chinatown: A Book of Pictures by Arnold Genthe*, Mitchell Kennerley, New York, 1908.

Lee, Calvin, *Chinatown, U.S.A.*, Doubleday & Company, New York, 1965.

McLeod, Alexander, *Pigtails and Gold Dust*, Caxton Printers, Ltd., Caldwell, Idaho, 1949.

Nee, Victor G.; and Nee, Brett de Bary, *Longtime Californ': A Documentary Study of an American Chinatown*, Houghton Mifflin Company, Boston, 1974.

Odo, (Dr.) Franklin Shoichiro, *In Movement: A Pictorial History of Asian America*, Visual Communications/Asian American Studies Center, Los Angeles, 1977.

Stellman, Louis J., *Mother Lode*, Harr Wagner Company, San Francisco, 1934.

Sun, Shirley, *Three Generations of Chinese—East and West*, Oakland Museum, Oakland, 1973.

Sung, Betty Lee, *Mountain of Gold*, Macmillan Company, New York, 1967.

Tow, J. S., *The Real Chinese in America*, Academy Press, New York, 1923.

Tung, William L., *The Chinese in America, 1820–1973: A Chronology and Fact Book*, Oceana Publications, Dobbs Ferry, New York, 1974.

UCLA Asian American Studies Center, *Roots: An Asian American Reader*, University of California, Los Angeles, 1971.

Wilson, Carol Green, *Chinatown Quest*, Stanford University, Stanford, 1931.

ARTICLES, PAMPLHETS AND MANUSCRIPTS

Beale, Truxtun, "Why the Chinese Should be Excluded," *Forum*, March 1902.

Business Week, "China's Own," September 4, 1943.

Coolidge, Mary Roberts, "Chinese Labor Competition on the Pacific Coast," *Annals of the American Academy of Political and Social Science*, September 1909.

Dillon, Richard H., "Louis J. Stellman's Chinatown," *American West*, January–February 1978.

Dresden, Donald, "L'autre Haute," *Washington Post Magazine*, May 7, 1978.

Fitch, G. K., papers, volume 1, Bancroft Library, Berkeley.

George, Henry, "Why Work Is Scarce, Wages Low, and Labor Restless: A Lecture," delivered in Metropolitan Temple, San Francisco, March 26, 1878, California Historical Society Library, San Francisco.

Gong, Edmond, "I Want to Marry an American Girl," *American Magazine*, September 1955.

Hauser, Ernest O., "Chinaman's Chance," *Saturday Evening Post*, December 7, 1940.

Hill, Herbert, "Anti-Oriental Agitation and the Rise of Working-Class Racism," *Society*, January–February 1973.

Hutcheson, Robert, "Why the Chinese Should be Admitted," *Forum*, March 1902.

Hutchings, James Mason, diary, 1855, Bancroft Library, Berkeley.

"The Invalidity of the 'Queue Ordinance' of the City and County of San Francisco: Opinion of the Circuit Court of the U.S. for the District of California in Ho Ah Kow vs. Matthew Nunan," July 7, 1879, California Historical Society Library, San Francisco.

Laughlin, (Rev.) John Hood, "Chinese Children in American Schools," *Overland Monthly*, May 1911.

Lee, Rose Hum, "The Decline of Chinatowns in the United States," *American Journal of Sociology*, March 1949.

Lindsey, David, "Cathay Comes to El Dorado," *American History Illustrated*, July 1975.

Manion, John J., papers, 1926–1946, Bancroft Library, Berkeley.

Morris, George B., "The Chinaman as He is," Bancroft Library, Berkeley.

Newsweek, "The Gangs of Chinatown," July 2, 1973.

Robbins, (Mrs.) E. V., "Chinese Slave Girls," *Overland Monthly*, January 1908.

Sayre, J. G., "More Chinese Atrocities," *Nation*, August 10, 1927.

Small, Sidney Herschel, "No Blood on the Streets of Chinatown," *Saturday Evening Post*, September 27, 1947.

Smith, William C., "Born American, But—", *Survey*, May 1926.

Stellman, Louis J., "Yellow Journals—San Francisco's Oriental Newspapers," *Sunset*, February 1910.

Time, "Chinaman's Chance," September 8, 1967.

Time, "The Chinatown Detail," September 28, 1970.

Wolfe, Tom, "The New Yellow Peril," *Esquire*, December 1969.

Wong, Jade Snow, "Growing Up Between the Old World and the New," *Hornbook*, December 1951.

Yee, Min, "Chinatown in Crisis," *Newsweek*, February 23, 1970.

Yoneda, Karl G., "A Brief History of U.S. Asian Labor," *Political Affairs*, September 1976.